KNOWING
WHICH END IS UP

PRACTICAL WISDOM THAT
REFRESHES THE HEART AND SOUL

DIANE SLONECKER

Unless otherwise indicated, Bible quotations are taken from:

New American Standard Version copyright © 1901 by Moody Press

NIV International Bible Society, copyright © 1973, 1978, 1984 by International Bible Society

King James by American Bible Society

New Layman's Parallel Bible, copyright © 1981 by Zondervan

Living Webster Encyclopedia Dictionary, copyright © 1981, 1980, 1977, 1975, 1973, 1972 and 1971, by DeLalir Publishing Strong's Exhaustive Concordance reprinted in 1985 by Baker Book House Co.

ISBN: 979-8-88640-532-3 (sc)
ISBN: 979-8-88640-533-0 (hc)
ISBN: 979-8-88640-534-7 (e)

Because of the dynamic nature of the Internet, any web addresses or links contained in this book may have changed since publication and may no longer be valid. The views expressed in this work are solely those of the author and do not necessarily reflect the views of the publisher, and the publisher hereby disclaims any responsibility for them.

THE EWINGS
PUBLISHING

One Galleria Blvd., Suite 1900, Metairie, LA 70001
1-888-421-2397

CONTENTS

Section I
Knowing Which End Is UP

Section II
Knowing Your Enemy

ACKNOWLEDGEMENTS

The more I write, the more I realize how many people have, in some way, contributed to my efforts including:

Ruth Carlson—Bless you pulling this all together by designing, formatting and helping me prepare this book for publication.

Carol Vogel—Thank you for giving so much prayer filled time and effort to the process of encouraging, critiquing, editing, and formatting.

Randal Greenfield, Julie Fields and Beth Kaedings—Thank you for blessing us through the sharing of your time and artistic talents.

Pastor Bill Hybels, Carol Beals, Winn Couchman, my husband, my children & their families, relatives, many special friends, acquaintances & even strangers—Thank you for all the ways you have touched and blessed my life and thus my writings.

The Staff at Xulon Press—Thank you for helping me give my writings wings.

My Lord Jesus—Thank you for sharing Yourself with me…gifting me with something of You…to share with others.

To my readers—May you be blessed by taking time to consider these writings.

INTRODUCTION

As an avid reader, I have often found myself concerned by people or writers who assess problems by assuming answers. Because experience has taught me that sharing false assumptions can be deadly.

Another style of writer or personality that can tend to leave me apprehensive, are ones who seem to have only overly-glowing descriptions of themselves in the midst of crisis or pain. I find myself wondering how they have managed to avoid facing the very real threat of fear and discouragement.

This book is written to those who, though they may have tried to live a good life, have tasted…or will taste…the struggle, discouragement or pain that can come with learning. Coming to recognize and apply divine wisdom is a mutual, life long process… with many divinely designed blessings worth sharing. May this book validate, stimulate, and encourage you!

Section I

Knowing Which End Is UP

1

In The Beginning. . .

As my little frame nestled under the bed covers seeking their warmth and comfort, I could hear it starting again. At first the words sounded far away and dim. But soon they began to feel like enormous angry waves pounding against jagged rocks. The roaring sounds eroded my sense of comfort and security. And I remember longing to hear the stormy ocean of words become calm and beautiful again…like when a huge golden sunset settles over a stilled sea.

Words have always had a profound effect on me. Even when I was far too young to understand their meaning, I was being affected by their tone. And now, many years later, a lifetime of words continue to wash over the shoreline of my mind. And as waves of past conversations crest, they then spread bubbling memories out in front of me…memories that continue to grow in meaning and value.

2

Growing Without Knowing

As a child I was raised with many good "Christian" principals, and I willingly embraced the idea that an All Powerful and Sovereign God loved and cared for me. But at the same time I felt a lot of confusion…about how or why evil often seemed to win out over good in so many situations around me. I knew I was trying and that those around me were trying to be loving and good. So then, why was there still so much cruelty and pain? "How is it that good or loving intentions could be so hurtful?" I wondered.

As I looked for answers to these problems from peers, parents and pastors, I was offered quite an assortment of well-intentioned assessments and instructions. "You're just making too much out of it!" "They didn't mean it!", (therefore, it really didn't hurt you). "We're not supposed to judge others!" "Just try to overlook it!" "Don't be negative!" "Forgive and forget!" "Think positive!" All of their observations seemed to fall into two main categories: I was the reason I saw problems, or there really were no problems.

So, though I lived amidst people who advocated and embraced God's unconditional love, I lived in an atmosphere that offered little more than humanistic evaluations of life's problems…and "common sense" cures for them (Colossians 2:8). And as I grew…away from childhood and towards adulthood…it became more and more apparent that life required more wisdom than I possessed.

As the pain of poor choice left me yearning to know how to successfully navigate the difficulties of life, I pursued a deeper search for guidance. But as I did I found that parents, teachers, counselors and leaders differed greatly about what they believed, especially in what they believed about God. "Will the real God please stand up… so I can see You for myself?" I found myself asking. "Lord, I've been sincerely trying to live the Christian life, but I must be missing something…please help me to see what it is I'm not understanding!" (Luke 11:9-10: Matthew 4:4)

Fortunately, God graciously heard my prayer…and began answering it!

3

Lord, I'm Scared!

Conflict and fear may not be comfortable, but their discomfort can prove to be very valuable motivation. They can stimulate us to try things that we have never tried before. They can push us to look for answers.

Because fear was one of my earliest companions, whenever I was scared I would try to take my fears to the God that I had been taught about. My first memory of "trying to talk to God" was when I was still pretty little, and was motivated by the familiar sound of angry voices arguing again. It always felt so scary to me. So one day, in order to escape the sounds of the conflict, I retreated to my bedroom closet, closed the door, and poured my little heart out to God. Later I learned that what I was doing was called "prayer", and that it was not only OK, it was advisable!

When I got older I learned to express my prayer-filled thoughts on paper. It seemed to help when I would write down what I was feeling. You could say that it sort of helped me "see" what I was thinking. And I noticed that my emotions seemed to become more manageable when I could get them on paper. Then, I could re-read them later, to get a more accurate perspective about what I had experienced.

Did you ever notice how much easier it is to write about a particular struggle after you have a victory? Because then you can emphasize the victory while diminishing the struggle, or you can emphasize the struggle and give a glowing account of how well you handled it.

But writing…writing honestly…shows that victories come tough sometimes. Perhaps because while victory seems to be the goal, the process is actually the product. All of life seems to be targeted toward producing a series of (gradual) changes that are designed to grow us or move us forward.

Often it takes an act of faith to risk moving forward. And learning to walk in faith is like learning to walk on water; no matter how you go about it, it never feels like solid ground! So we need something solid under us to keep us afloat…while we question, investigate, and discover.

"Call to Me and I will answer you,
and I will tell you great and mighty
things, which you do not know."

Jeremiah 33:3

4

Who Knows?

Dr. Albert Einstein, generally considered to be one of the great scientists of all time said, "My religion consists of a humble admiration of the illimitable superior Spirit who reveals Himself in the slight detail we are able to perceive with our frail and feeble minds. That deeply emotional conviction of the incomprehensible universe forms my idea of God."

Dr. Einstein thus shared with us how he was able to identify God's power and presence in nature. Unfortunately, his statement shed no light on how we might get in touch with that God…or how we might know what God's agenda might be. "Why did God create life?" I wondered. "And what does He want me to do with the gift of life He has given me?"

Addressing such questions, I came to realize that I was attempting to believe in a God I didn't really know. I was trying to live a faith that had been given to me by my parents. It wasn't *my* faith, because faith is an assurance…a conviction. What I had was someone else's conviction…a "hand-me-down" faith. How was I to develop my own faith…my own convictions? How could I know for sure if what I had been taught about God was really true?

Know—To be able to distinguish or
differentiate; To have knowledge, or clear
and certain perception, as of fact of truth.

5

Do I Know You?

Perhaps out of a desire to promote a sense of unity, we often hear an emphasis on the similarity of world religions. This emphasis may even draw people to naively assume that all religions are basically the same. It's true that many advocate the "Golden Rule" in various forms. The idea being that we should treat others, as we ourselves would like to be treated and somehow, as long as we're trying to do the right thing, we'll be okay. Often this principal of trying to be good is wrongly assumed to be the very essence of Christianity. But trying to be good or struggling to please God constitutes "religion", not "Christianity". Much like psychology and philosophy, religion is man's attempt to reach the unknown. Whereas Christianity…is God taking the initiative to reach out to unknowing man…to offer him a personal relationship…through which man can come to know and trust Him.

Imagine, if you will, my coming up to you and saying, "Tim or Mary (or whatever your name is), "I want you to trust me!" Can you imagine your reply? It is bound to be something like, "Well gee, I don't even know you! How can you expect me to trust you when I don't even know you!"

Do you suppose that this might be what some of us have tried to do with God? Are we trying to trust God without ever really getting to know Him?

10 FT.
10 FT.
10 FT

6

Wanting To Know

It has been said that "Faith without fact is fanaticism in action." That is because faith without fact is but "emotional hoping".... hoping in hope! We hear people say that they are "hoping for the best" or that they are "hoping beyond all hope." What they are actually hoping is that there is some kind of power in the act of hoping. Because they know that hopelessness is an enemy that they need to say "no" to!

But the antidote for hopelessness is not vain hoping; rather it is accurate knowing. We need to "know" what the truth is, so that we can say "no" to what is not.

God has said, "My people are destroyed for lack of knowledge" (Hosea 4:6). God's Word warns us that destruction comes not from the lack of effort...not from the lack of love...but from the lack of accurate knowing. Without knowing what is true, hopelessness can defeat us as we try and try again, only to fail and fail again. Or it can defeat us when we don't try at all, because we don't know where to begin. Or it can set us up for disaster by leading us to take a misdirected flying leap, that is based on a blind faith.

God is not calling us to live in blind faith. He is calling us to look at His Truth. Then we can walk in the protection of it!

"He created everything there is…
nothing exists that He didn't make."

John 1:3

7

A Source We Can Trust

When we look at the beauty and wonder of our universe, we see an incredible array of complex and diverse life forms. All of creation introduces us to magnificent examples of design, organization, and efficiency…which reflect the value and power of forethought, while evidencing a deliberately planned or created order. Recognized or not…all things have purposely designed power or effect.

God's Word reveals *our* purposely designed power or effect, as it explains that mankind is the vehicle God designed…to express and extend Himself to…and through. It informs us that when God created you and me, He molded and shaped valuable pieces of His own character and ability into us. But God's Word also clarifies that though we have been created in God's image…we are not God…we are therefore less than God.

As we begin to understand the opportunity as well as the vulnerability of our position, we begin to appreciate that God has designed an incredibly wise plan for the parenting of His creation. But the design requires His willingness to suffer its process.

The idea of God suffering is new for some. Because we imagine that if we were in God's position of power, we would use that position to protect ourselves from all pain or discomfort, not give ourselves to it. But God knew what it would take to bring His creation to completion. It would require God's righteous energy to infuse light into the darkness…God's wisdom and patience to teach the immature…God's strength of character to prevail over the enticement of evil.

Cleave—(Hebr.) dabaq- cling, adhere, cleave
Cleave—(Webster) to be attached; to adhere to

8

God Our Creator

Some of the specifics of how humanity was created are described in the Bible, second chapter of Genesis: "Then the Lord formed man of dust from the ground, and breathed into his nostrils the breath of life; and the man became a living being. And the Lord God planted a garden toward the east, in Eden; and there He placed the man whom He had formed (Genesis 2:7-8). Then the Lord God took the man and put him into the garden of Eden to cultivate it and keep it. And the Lord commanded the man, saying, 'From any tree of the garden you may eat freely; but from the tree of the knowledge of good and evil you shall not eat, for in the day that you eat from it you shall surely die.' *Then (emphasis mine)* the Lord God said, 'It is not good for the man to be alone; I will make a helper suitable for him' (Genesis 2:15-18). So the Lord God caused a deep sleep to fall upon the man, and he slept; then He took one of his ribs, and closed up the flesh at that place." "And the Lord God fashioned into woman the rib which He had taken from man, and brought her to the man. And the man said, 'This is now bone of my bone, and flesh of my flesh; She shall be called Woman, because she was taken out of Man.' For this cause a man shall leave his father and his mother, and shall cleave to his wife; and they shall become one flesh. And the man and his wife were both naked and were not ashamed" (Genesis 2:21-25).

From these verses we see that God designed man and woman to fit together and function collectively. Because a piece of himself was now missing in man, God warned that it was "not good" for man to be independent. Instead, man was to "cleave" to that enhanced "missing piece" that God had fashioned into the form of "woman."

We are also given to see through these verses that both the man and the woman were, at that point, feeling no self-consciousness or shame in the freedom of their shared vulnerability or exposure. So then what happened to that Divine creation of mutual paradise or bliss?

9

Paradise…Lost

Endowed with God's image and privileged to live in Paradise, Adam and Eve had been entrusted with tremendous opportunity for contentment. The only restriction given them was the warning that they were not to eat of the one tree that would bring about their destruction, the tree of the knowledge of good and evil. So we can conclude that Adam and Eve were innocent or ignorant about the distinction between good and evil. Their innocence therefore needed to be protected. Their free will meant that they could choose to listen to God or not. But their innocence left them ignorant about the consequences of ignoring God's protective limits. They had yet to understand the value of restraint. Chapter three of Genesis tells how Adam and Eve were lured away from taking God at His Word. The serpent (appealing to Eve's freedom to choose) suggested to her that God's restrictions were unfair, and that God's intention was to deprive her of something desirable.

Why did the serpent make this suggestion to Eve first instead of to Adam? Well, according to the account given in Genesis 2:16-22, Eve was not yet created from Adam's rib when God commanded Adam not to eat of the forbidden tree. We are not told how Eve was made aware of the restriction. But we see in Genesis 3:1-3 that apparently she had some awareness of it. Yet the serpent is seen to be successful in deceiving her into believing that there would be a very desirable outcome if she would listen to him (the serpent) instead of God.

So Eve not only ate the forbidden fruit herself, she gave some to Adam as well. And we read (vs.6) that Adam took it and ate it. There is no record of Adam trying to refuse it, or of Adam trying to warn Eve away from eating, even though God had addressed the issue very clearly and specifically with him (2:16). Both Adam and Eve were then faced with the deadly consequences of exercising their free will in direct opposition to God's protective directive.

Wrong choices, then as now, resulted in deadly consequences. The truth is what it is…whether we know it…or believe…or not!

10

You Know Not

The pain that is caused by our ignorance is a manifestation of imperfection. It is evidence of our human falleness. When God birthed you and me into this world, He knew He was sending us into, and as a part of, a society of creatures who were not (omniscient) all knowing. Suffering and pain reflect our human inability to be perfect…to always make the best choice…each and every time that we have the opportunity.

Yet the pain of imperfection serves us, as it awakens us to the value of rightness, the superiority of Perfection. Pain and suffering educate us about the consequences of misusing our "free will". We are not born with a disposition to automatically choose rightly. But we are born with the capacity of conscience, the ability to distinguish right from wrong, constructive from destructive, good from lack of good. However, we also possess the ability to override our conscience. But when we do, we come to the experience of a very special, Divinely designed warning system…called guilt.

"What shall we say then? Is the Law sin? May it never be! On the contrary, I would not have come to know sin except through the Law; for I would not have known about covet-ing if the Law had not said, "YOU SHALL NOT COVET."

Romans 7:7

11

Discovering Guilt

In the third chapter of Genesis we read the first account of man and woman experiencing something that did not feel good to them. Here we see that when Adam and Eve deviated from God's instructions, and therefore, "did eat" of the forbidden fruit, "Then the eyes of both of them were opened, and they realized they were naked" (which means bare or exposed) (Genesis 3:7). Actually, they had always been naked. But now, suddenly, after disobeying God, being bare or exposed felt uncomfortable to them. So next, we see them attempting to cover their new sense of shame or embarrassment with fig leaves.

Also for the first time, we see Adam and Eve trying to hide from God. They had come to experience the consequence of disobedience, the emotional pain of guilt, which kept them from feeling comfortable in God's presence. But instead of humbly turning to God as His light was shone on their error, they reacted by seeking to blame God—and one another—for their discomfort. And though the "serpent" was finally identified as the source of the temptation, each of them was seen to have had the chance to refuse the invitation to disobey God. But they did not…because neither the man nor the woman knew when to say "no"!

"...But to this one I will look,
To him who is humble and contrite of
spirit, and who trembles at My Word."

Isaiah 66:2

12

Condemnation vs. Conviction

I'm not going to feel guilty about this, because I am forgiven."
In some situations such a statement could be appropriate. But
in other circumstances it might be the result of refusing to take
responsibility for the destructiveness of our sin. In order to qualify
when such an attitude is healthy…or not, we need to clarify the
difference between condemnation and conviction.

Condemnation means: sentenced to damnation, eternal
punishment, hell; sentenced to the abode of evil, torment, or misery.
But conviction means: coming to see the truth; the state of being
convinced; an act of recognition. Romans 8:1 assures us that "There
is now no condemnation for those who are in Christ Jesus". But God's
Word does not say that there is no conviction for those in Christ.
As a matter of fact, there must be a coming to see… a conviction of
our own sinfulness…before we can experience forgiveness. We have
to see and acknowledge our condition before we can receive God's
provision for it.

When Jesus came to this earth, His "goodness" stood in sharp
contrast to "badness". So His righteous life exposed the presence, as
well as the vehicle, of evil. Wouldn't you have expected that when
Jesus exposed the existence of such a threatening condition, people
would have appreciated His warning?

Well some did. Some acknowledged the evil as they were given
to see it, and proclaimed their desire for righteousness. They became
personally "convicted" of their sinfulness. But then, why is it, that

others did not become convicted or convinced of the truth they were being shown? Was it because they...

P ... Pretended that they were not vessels of sin in order to
R ... rid themselves of the embarrassment and shame that are a natural result of sin...
I ... Instead of admitting their personal guilt, did they
D ... decide to
E ... establish standards that would allow and encourage the acceptance of their sin?

When man does this, he is in fact, attempting to usurp God's authority...by seeking to negate God's standards.

13

Permissivism vs. Grace

Have you ever tried to put something together without the benefit of the instructions…like a child's bicycle… on Christmas Eve?! Or have you ever gotten lost while driving your car someplace…and been bound and determined to find your way without looking at a map or stopping to ask for directions?

"If all else fails, read the directions", is a "common sense" suggestion. What is it in us that likes to "prove" that we can "do it" without anyone "telling us how"?

In giving us a free will God has given us the opportunity to make personal choices. But along with the gift of personal choice, He offers us directions or instructions concerning those choices. God's Truth empowers us to know ahead of time what will work, or how something works. But in our "humanness" we may view those instructions as a challenge. We may even attempt to "prove" that what "God says" is somehow not true in our case. And when we have this attitude, how does God deal with us? Does He force us to obey Him? Or, does He allow us to become convinced of His Truth through the experience of our disobedience? Disobedience produces loss…and some losses are very terribly costly…to ourselves as well as to others. And that's the point God wants us to see…the cost! Sometimes it takes a long time for the "cost" of something to surface. But if, when God shows us our costly disobedience, we acknowledge it, seeking His counsel and forgiveness, we will come to the true experience of God's Amazing Grace! However, if we refuse to "look at" what God is inviting us to see, we will miss the opportunity of His Grace…and will be left to the task of trying to rationalize our choices in order to permissively indulge ourselves in sin's temporary gratifications or relief. Any time we do this, we are, in effect, calling God a liar…and permitting ourselves to play god.

God does not condone self appointed, self anointed disobedience, because such unrighteous behavior is deadly. Yet in allowing it, He uses it…to bring us to the realization of our need to become free of it. God uses that which is evil, to bring us to value that which is good. Now, that's Amazing!…That's Grace!

14

Taking God At His Word

The Bible teaches that:

- ❑ We are all born fallen.
  (Psalm 51:5; Romans 3:20)

- ❑ We need to realize and grieve the effects of our falleness because that's what brings us to the desire for righteousness. *(Matt.5:6; 2 Cor.7:10 ; Acts 17:30)*

- ❑ We need to realize and understand our inability to attain righteousness by our own efforts because that's what leads us to recognize our need to be rescued.
  (Galations 3:21-24)

God's Word informs us that the opportunity to become rescued or "saved" from sin and its consequences comes through "receiving" or "believing" on Jesus Christ (*John 3:16*). The Greek word for believe is, *pisteuo* (pist-yoo'-o)...*to entrust one's self to; commit to; consistently rely on in fidelity. (fidelity – adherence to fact or truth).*

Receiving or believing on Jesus to be our personal Savior and Lord means taking Him into our heart in a volitional choice to put Him before self...to choose to defer control of the power, status, and independence that God has given us, back to Him. Therefore when Jesus the Christ has been received into a person's life, His presence there becomes very evident...as that person's "choices" begin to manifest a new kind of Divine Influence!

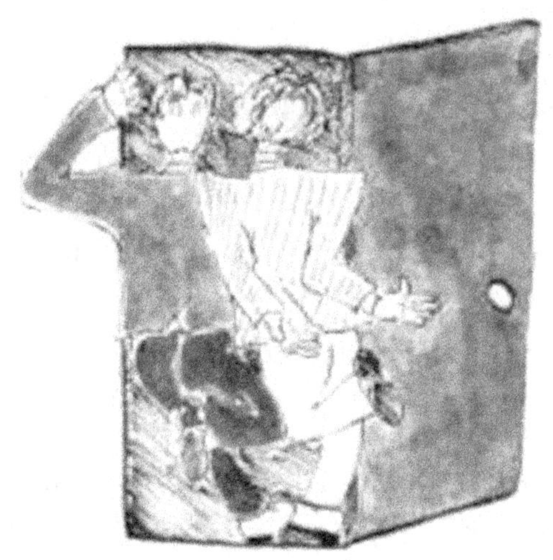

15

Why In The World Would You Do That?!

Imagine if you will for a moment…two people meeting at a narrow doorway. As they both realize that they cannot fit going through it at the same time, one person steps back to say to the other, "You go first". But instead of going first, the other person says, "No, you go first". Here we have an example of the first person giving the second person "preference" or opportunity. Then we see that "preferred" person take that gift of preference or opportunity and choose to use it, to offer preference back to the one who offered it to him in the first place.

Now in much the same way, The Lord Jesus says to us, "Here, I give you life. I give you power, status, and independence. I give you opportunity…even the opportunity to be free of Me…free from My Righteousness (Romans 6:20)!" But after we realize what the Lord is offering us, we are then in a position to "choose" to say to Him, "No, I give You my life, Lord. I relinquish the opportunity You have given me to be independent of You, because I *want* You to be the Lord of my life. I see that being united with You is more valuable than being independent of You! I value Your value to me! Therefore, I defer the control of my life to You, because I have come to understand and appreciate You as my Ultimate Source…and Resource! (Romans 6:3-23)

16

Coming To Know...

Becoming a Christian can be an ego shattering experience at first, as it exposes our imperfection and inability to save our selves. Yet it is the solid foundation of self-esteem, as we come to understand our true value and importance from God's perspective.

Even as a child I understood that I was a sinner. Even as a child I desired to be free of that sin; I wanted Jesus to be my Savior. And even as a child I was taught about grace. But it wasn't until I was an adult that I came to learn how those pieces fit together. It wasn't until I was an adult that I came to really understand and experience true forgiveness. Because it wasn't until I was an independent and free willed adult, with obvious sin in my life, that I was really able to "see", "understand", and "admit" my condition.

In true Biblical Christianity, once we have realized our sin and we desire to become free of it, our next step is to understand our own inability to get rid of it. Romans 3:19-20 explains that the revelation of God's Law is the very thing that exposes our inability to keep it. That's why carnal man becomes so irritated by having God's standard of perfection held up to him. Because it proves him to be the very thing he is trying to deny. Our "sinful passions are aroused by the law" because we resent having a standard of behavior held up to us that seems impossible (Romans 7:5; John 3:20). So then, having Jesus Christ held up as an example of the ability to be "human yet sinless" can lead us to want to cry out…"Well He was God!…but I'm only human!"

"If you love Me, obey Me; and I will ask the Father and He will give you another Comforter, and He will never leave you. He is the Holy Spirit, the Spirit who leads into all truth. The world at large cannot receive Him, for it isn't looking for Him and doesn't recognize Him."

John 14:15-17

17

"No Wonder!"

The term "only human" is a very accurate description of the life that is not voluntarily attached to Jesus. Because only as His Holy Spirit resides in us are we empowered to recognize and implement spiritual truths (1Corinthians 2:9-14).

Without God's Holy Spirit empowering us, our human nature just isn't able to understand the horrible hold that sin has on us. So as a child that was raised to be held accountable for my behavior, yet not able to identify spirituals truths, I struggled to understand why or how my will power had failed to keep me from "sin", because I was trying…I was really trying…yet failing at times. But it was my failure that finally brought me to cry out for God in utter helplessness. And even though I had considered myself a Christian my whole life, it was only as I recognized and acknowledged my total dependency on God that He began to reveal Himself to me (2Corinthians 3:16).

Why is this step of "crying uncle" so necessary? Because it is what changes our heart from prideful (trying to be okay) and resistive (afraid of not being okay) to being grateful, in awe of God's amazing grace…yet able to feel penitent as God lovingly and patiently leads us to see our condition.

As I came to see the imperfection or falleness of human nature, I realized that I would have already been completely destroyed by all the sin in this world, except for God's compassionate hand of staying grace. And as my mind realized the reason for my Lord's compassion I whispered…"No wonder!"…"No wonder I couldn't do it by myself!"

"There is a way which seems right to a man, But its end is the way of death."

Proverbs 16:25

18

Sin...What is it?

The Greek word, *hamartano*, which we translate as *sin*, is a word whose definition suggests the idea of *"missing the mark"...and in so doing... "not sharing the prize"*. Webster defines it as the willful departure from Divine Law.

Over the years I've come to see that there is a lot of controversy about how the law should or shouldn't interfere with free will. We want to feel free to make our own choices, but we don't necessarily understand our own vulnerabilities. We want to be able to feel secure. But we may not understand just what it takes to feel secure in a society endowed with free will.

How do free will and security fit together? Security comes from having the opportunity to be protected from harm. While free will actually allows the opportunity for harm. Because though I can choose to comply with God's protective directives, I cannot force anyone else to. Others may actually make choices that are very hurtful to me. Now if their choices could only hurt them, we might see that as justice. But when their choices hurt others, we call it unfair; we call it cruelty or victimization. Yet why are such choices being made?...Why did Adam and Eve make such an ignorant and hurtful choice that has affected the world ever since (Genesis 3)?

19

Truth and Consequences

The consequence of being given the truth is that we are thereby given a choice as to how we will respond. We can take the truth or leave it. But if truth is withheld from us, we have no choice but to function without adequate protection from error. "Protective Directives" are what make free will possible.

Freedom of choice means that we have the freedom or opportunity to decide who or what to believe. We can choose to believe that what God says is true, or what someone else says is true. We can take God at His Word, or not. No matter what the issue and no matter how many differing opinions can be heard on an issue, our choice will be the same: to side with God, or not. "He who is not with me is against me; and he who does not gather with me scatters" (Matthew 12:30).

Why would anyone in their right mind choose to oppose God? Did Adam and Eve think they were "defying God"? Did they think they were choosing something hurtful to themselves? Did they think that they knew better than God? Or did they not understand that they had an enemy that they needed to be protected from? And did they not realize that God's limits brought protection, not deprivation?

Adam and Eve were experiencing total freedom and contentment when they were placed in the Garden of Eden. They had no fear of evil, no awareness of any possibility of pain, because they had never experienced it, nor had they seen anyone else experience it. They felt capable. They were bearers of God's image, so they were experiencing some of God's own power and strength. And even though God had warned them that they would die if they ate of the forbidden fruit, what did those words mean to them? After all, they had never seen death.

Only ***after*** disobeying God did they come to realize the cost of deviating from His Words. Only ***after*** rejecting His counsel did they come to understand the protection of it! They had been entrusted with power and strength. Yet they knew not how it could work against them instead of for them!

20

Choose!

"Do you want what's behind curtain number one, curtain number two, or curtain number three?", asked the TV show host. The contestant was then expected to pick one of the three curtains. The audience could sometimes see what was behind a curtain, but the contestant could not. That was the agenda of a very popular and long-standing TV show. And when I used to watch that show, I often found myself wishing that some contestant would address the proposed "choice" being offered them by saying something like, "Well please tell me what's behind each curtain so that I can then "choose" one of them. How can this be called a "choice" when you don't tell me what my "choices" really are?"

Well, all the years I watched that show I never saw any contestant voice that response. They all just picked a curtain, contents unseen, and hoped for the best. They made a stab in the dark, hoping they would not end up with something they did not want.

As we think about it, how many of our so-called choices in life are made like those on that old TV show...blindly? How many times do we try to "choose" without really knowing the value, or lack of value, of our choice? How many of our choices become a disappointment – or worse yet, a disaster...because we didn't see hidden consequences?

What does it take to be able to make good choices? What brings us to realize the advantages, as well as the disadvantages, of having the opportunity to make our own choices? Never did it become so critically important for me to know the answers to such questions than when I became a parent. It was then, of course, that I came to realize that raising a child to use, yet not abuse their "freedom of choice" was no small task. And as a parent I came face to face with another challenge…that of knowing just how and when to use my own ability to choose, to direct or even override my children's choices. Sometimes my interventions were seen as helpful and perhaps even gave them a sense of security, while other times they were no doubt viewed as hindrances. I wanted my children to be free to learn and discover things for themselves. Yet what was I to do about things like **eating the poison of forbidden fruit**! Some things they could afford to live and learn, but other things threatened to **rob them of life** before they could learn!

21

"It's My Life, And I Can Do Whatever I Want With It!"

Have you ever heard those words from someone dear to you? Or have you ever said them yourself? What kind of picture is formed in your mind when you think about them? And what kinds of feelings do you think these words tend to solicit?

If you picture a young person saying these words to a parent, for instance, you might imagine that young person desiring something that the parent is warning them against. You might even see that young person feeling "controlled" and, therefore, wanting to feel free to make their own choices. So their argument may seem logical as you relate it to their sense of suppression.

But now, if you turn that picture around and visualize yourself as the parent on the receiving end of those words, what feelings can you see yourself having? Do you picture yourself merely feeling irritated at having your authority questioned? Or can you imagine yourself feeling the painful effects of wisdom, as you seek to warn your child away from the dangers that come with the circumstances?

Youth longs to discover, while maturity desires to protect the process of discovery.

"Be sober, be vigilant; because your adversary the devil, as a roaring lion, walketh about, seeking whom he may devour."

1 Peter 5:8

22

Obedience Is A Choice

I'm sure I'm not alone in identifying with the old saying, "Old too soon…smart too late". Yet, as I continue to grow and learn, I continue to grow in appreciation for God's wisdom. How wise is His design of bringing us to the truth through the avenue of free will. Because that way, obedience to God's protective limits is a choice that we make when we come to realize the harmfulness of its alternative…sin.

Sin (choosing other than God's design) is a deceiver. It offers us the "fly now pay later plan" as it urges us toward immediate gratification, while denying the reality of destructive consequences. Sin clothes itself in appealing sights, sounds, sensations, and smiles. But sin lies…sin kills…sin robs us of God's designed best (John 10:10).

But as we can see from the example of Adam and Eve, naive human nature is no match for the sneaky snake's ability to enslave our minds by deception. So we need more than humanistic wisdom, more than mere common sense. We need Divine Guidance. We need to know how to recognize and utilize God's Supernatural (more than merely human) protective directives. Because our enemy is diabolic!

"Truth, ever lovely—since the world began...
The foe of tyrants, and the friend of man."

Thomas Campbell
Pleasures of Hope Pt ii

23

The Truth Lights Our Way

How comfortable are you with the truth? Do you tend to see it as your friend or as your enemy? Most of us are probably familiar with the saying; "Sometimes the truth hurts". Do you agree? And if so, how so? When does the truth hurt, and why?

"Truth, ever lovely – since the world began.
The foe of tyrants, and the friend of man."
Thomas Campbell
Pleasures of Hope Pt ii

Truth is what God uses (it is His intrinsic nature) to set us free from all bondag*e...* (John 1:14; John 14:6; Hosea 4:6*)...*and bring us to eternal paradise. On the other hand, lack of truth, distortion of truth, omission of truth, compromising truth, and the manipulation of truth, is what Satan uses (it is his intrinsic nature) to keep us in bondage...and bring us to eternal destruction (Revelations 12:9).

God invites, while Satan entraps...God reveals, while Satan conceals...God empowers, while Satan enslaves. God's concern is for "thee"...while Satan's concern is for "me"!

Egotism—a passionate and exaggerated love of self, lead-ing one to refer all things to oneself, and to judge everything by its relation to one's interest or importance.

24

"My Way" Becomes The Highway

Who is this person we refer to as Satan? How did he come to be God's enemy? And why doesn't God just step on him, like a bug, and there by eliminate him?!

The Hebrew word, Satan, means adversary. An adversary is an enemy, an opponent – someone having hostility for another. Isaiah 14 and Ezekiel 28 describe the heart of such an adversary. Here we see the "created" trying to put himself on the same level as God… trying to take all the ability and power that God had designed him to have, and acting as though it was his own doing. "You said in your heart, I will ascend to heaven; I will raise my throne above the stars of God…I will make myself like the most High" (Isaiah 14:13-14).

How could one of God's creatures acquire such an attitude? How could the creature spurn the very loving, powerful God that had created him…the God that had entrusted that creature with some of His (God's) own Beauty, Wisdom, and Power!

"Your heart was lifted up because of your beauty; you corrupted your wisdom by reason of your splendor" (Ezekiel 28:17). The being that God had created took all that God had given him and went on an "ego trip". "Look at me", he thought…"Look at how powerful I am"!

Satan came to defy God because he wanted to be God. He wanted to be in control. Thus he refused to submit to the Divine Design of his Creator. He refused to accept the fact that, though endowed with power *from* God, he was *not* God!

And how did God react to such arrogance? Well unlike us, God is not "threatened" by opposition. God knew from the beginning that, in allowing His creation to have free will, He was automatically allowing the potential for opposition. So, rather than squashing it like a bug, He uses it to prove or manifest the superior power, purpose and benefit of **His Righteousness.**

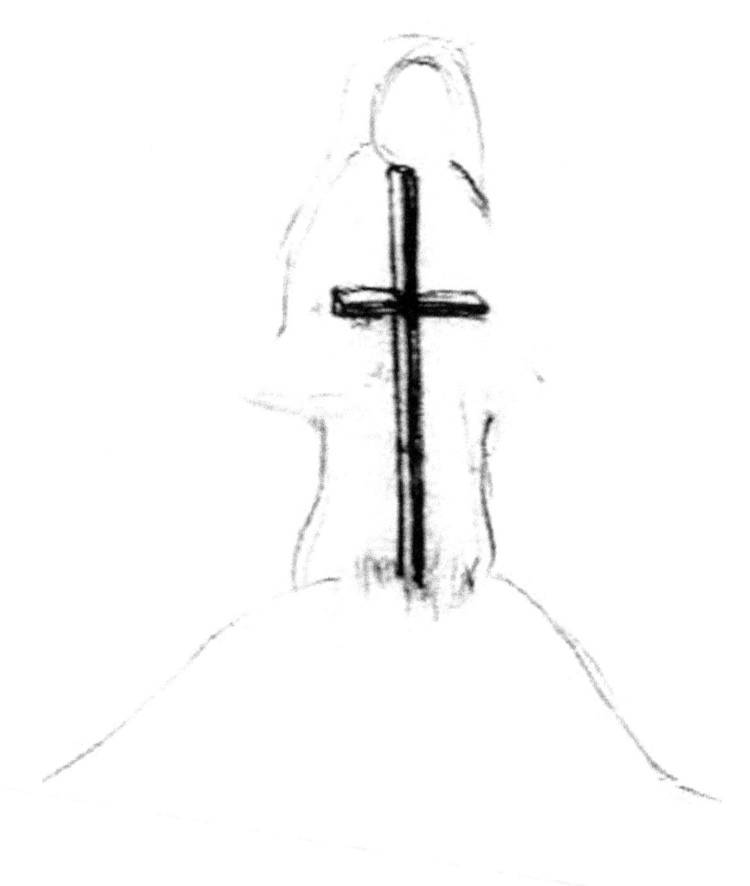

25

The Road To Heaven...or Hell

Out of a volitional choice, Jesus, God's own flesh and blood, relinquished the pomp and paradise of His heavenly throne, and entered this world through the avenue of humility. And though it certainly would have been appropriate for Him to Lord Himself over us, instead He lovingly and sacrificially identified Himself with us...roll modeling what He knew we needed to see.

In an incredible manifestation of Holy Union, Jesus showed us how life can be lived in connection with and surrendered to the righteousness of Divine Will. Even when doing right meant having to suffer the wrongs of others, Jesus chose to stand unitedly with His Heavenly Father, rather than dividedly from Him (John 7:7&16-18). He did this so that you and I could come to see how it is that sin, meaning anything outside of God's Righteous Design, will kill, rob, and destroy.

It was mankind's sin that put God's flesh and blood on a cross. It was mankind's sin that buried Divine Righteousness in a grave. But, Jesus the Ideal, could not be kept in the grave. Therefore, Jesus' torturous death, burial, then glorious resurrection, proved that though Satan be allowed the free will to take his best shot at usurping or destroying Righteousness, he cannot do it!

Out of love for us and fulfillment of His plan, God sent His own flesh and blood to earth to show us what Truth and Love look like lived out in the flesh. But as we were given to see, "living out the truth in love" can provoke tremendous jealousy in the human heart, because it exposes humanity's imperfection. So as Jesus' perfection brought recognition of man's falleness, some bowed in humble acknowledgment, while others clamored to kill the Ideal, Jesus. In the foolishness of sinful pride, some sought to discredit or eliminate the threat of righteousness. So even as Jesus offered them love and forgiveness, they retaliated with arrogance and hate! (Luke 23:20-23; Ephesians 5:2; John 13:34; &14:6; John 4:8 & 8:12)

Amazingly, God did not hire someone else to do this painful and dirty work of salvation. Rather He saved us Himself...coming in the flesh to suffer physical (natural) death...in order to offer us the Superior Power of Spiritual (supernatural) Life!

In order to free us from the hellish consequences of sin, Jesus, the Christ...God in human skin...suffered terribly, cruelly, unfairly, and sacrificially...thereby providing what He knew we could never accomplish for ourselves. Instead of simply designing us to be some kind of righteous robots, God chose a way of sharing Himself with us that would bring us to see our need of Him, while creating an avenue to Him. God's incredible design of life endowed with free will, meant that He would have to suffer with us and for us, in order to bring us to the understanding of what it takes to fully enjoy all that He offers us!

None of us really understand just how much we need God to be our God, until we see our human vulnerabilities. None of us possess the wisdom and skill to rightly use what God has entrusted to us, until we give God's Spirit the freedom to live in us...in order that He be free to live through us.

But this extraordinary privilege of having the Spirit of God living in us does not come to us except we voluntarily receive it, because God will not impose Himself on us. He *offers* us His Truth and Love. He does not force it on us. Yet, when in fear, ignorance or rebellion we refuse His Divine Guidance, God allows us to experience His absence...in order that we come to appreciate His presence (Jeremiah 29:11-13; Proverbs 8:17; Matthew 7:7-14).

Through an incredibly sacrificial yet thoroughly wise plan, God has provided a way for us to come to realize His value...as well as our potential value. He graciously brings us to see that connected to Him, we become accessible vessels of honor and blessing...while apart from Him, we become vessels of dishonor and loss (Timothy 2:15-26).

26

Knowing

Most of us do not get up in the morning with the idea that we are going to be instruments of harm or loss. We don't say to ourselves, "I'm going to do something really hurtful today". Yet some days we end up doing more harm than good. Because we may not understand the force of evil that is in this world, and what or "who" is needed to accomplish its agenda. Our enemy is very shrewd. He knows how to exploit our natural abilities. He is skilled at preying on our natural vulnerabilities. He may seek to lure us to feelings of dread or fear. Or he may lead us into believing we need have no fear.

As a child I yearned for a sense of security. As an adult I worked hard at seeking to achieve it. But it wasn't until I began to understand my enemy, that I found it. My security didn't come from being invincible. And it didn't come from being unaware. It came as I faced my own fallenness…in faith instead of despair. My enemy was not the recognition of sin. My enemy was and still is the misrepresentation of it…and therefore…the misunderstanding of it. God knows that loving someone does not mean ignoring or minimizing what is killing them.

Sin (meaning the acceptance of anything other than God's designed best) looses its power over us as it is confessed…and addressed. Yet as we begin to identify it, we may find that it has become a way of life for us. Because we are attempting to meet a very deep felt need through it, we may even feel "threatened" by the prospect of being expected to live without it. So we may choose, for ourselves and others, to simply accept it and develop the ability to rationalize it. But the trouble with rationalization is that it doesn't do what it is sent out to do. It doesn't free us, it enslaves us. It doesn't bless us, it curses…it dooms.

Have you ever really understood your own humanness? Have you come to appreciate its need? Have you ever actually taken that neediness to our Savior? Do you understand the freedom in taking Him at His Word? Our Creator has already made the choice of what He wants us to have. He wants to bring us to completion…the place of never ending blessedness. Now we have to decide whether or not we will receive it.

Remember God is the One who created you…out of a Love that we have yet to fully understand. He is inviting you to come to know Him…He is extending to you His gracious and loving hand. So reach out and take it…because…**Self-will** brings death…but **God's Will** brings life…everlasting!

Section II

Knowing Your Enemy

1

Shattered Dreams

It wasn't supposed to be like this! After so much effort and progress, how could I have failed so. What would I do now? How would I be able to handle everything?!

Each decision I had made felt like the right one at the time. And yet eventually, time and maturity would show me that many of those decisions had been based on faulty thinking or deceptive emotions.

But little by little, as the clouds began to part, I settled into my new life style. Even though life was now filled with new and difficult responsibilities, there was still a comfort that came with finding out that I could go on.

After several years that included mistakes and loss, I was finding that God was available to me in ways that I had never understood before. The changes in my life were many, some voluntary, some not. One of the things that had changed was the area in which I lived. So that meant finding a new church. But while I was attending a church that I felt my family might like, my then teenage son, became involved with a youth group that he had heard about at school. And through his association with this new found youth program, he wanted to go to *that* church on Sundays. Well, when my teenager wanted to get up early on a Sunday morning in order to go to some newly found church, I felt it my duty as a parent to check it out, fearing that it might be some kind of cult. So one Sunday I went there. The irony was that while I was so concerned about my son being misled, I had not yet come to recognize parts of my own lostness. So I was totally unprepared for what I was about to experience.

"...by the works of the Law no flesh will
be justified in His sight; for through the
Law comes the knowledge of sin".

Romans 3:20

2

The Approach Of New Life

It first the words were familiar. But then, just as I started to anticipate what was going to be said, I began to hear things I had never heard before. I was being told that I wasn't a sinner because I sinned, but that I sinned because I was a sinner. And as I sat there listening, I could sense a flood of warm tears becoming released from somewhere deep inside me. And as they steadily trickled down my face, I felt them washing away years of confusion and guilt.

"If a law had been given which was able to impart life, then righteousness would indeed have been based on the law. But Scripture has shut up all men under sin, that the promise by faith in Jesus Christ might be given to those who believe…"Therefore, the Law has become our tutor to lead us to Christ, that we may be justified by Christ" (Galations 3:21,22,24).

The words continued, but rather than hearing their sounds I found myself steeped in their meaning. Oh how well God knew just what I needed to hear. Only He could have arranged such welcomed relief. And before I left that place that day, I had a new understanding of the words "Amazing Grace".

God understood my ignorance. He knew that I didn't realize that…"by the works of the law no flesh will be justified in His sight; for through the Law comes the knowledge of sin (Rom.3:20). And God knew how alone I had felt in my guilt. So He assured me that we "**all** have sinned and fall short of the glory of God".

It was a relief to realize that fallenness wasn't just my problem, but that it was a human condition that **everyone** is faced with (Romans 3:23). And in recognizing the plight of my own human fallenness, I was so very appreciative of God's provision for my condition!

3

"Plop, Plop, Fizz, Fizz, Oh What A Relief It Is!"

When we are ailing, we greatly appreciate being able to ingest something that brings relief. And in our gratitude, we tend to want to tell others about the remedy we came to discover, because we know how desperately relief is needed in times of great pain. The release I found that day didn't come in the form of some pill, nor did it come from drinking some potion. It did however, come from ingesting something…it came from ingesting God's Word.

"The Word is near you, in your mouth and in your heart…that is, the Word of faith which we are preaching, that if you confess with your mouth Jesus as **Lord**, and believe in your heart that God raised Him from the dead, you shall be saved; for with the heart man believes, resulting in righteousness, and with the mouth he confesses, resulting in salvation" *(Romans 10:8-10).*

"The one who joins himself to the Lord is one spirit with Him" *(1Corinthians 6:17).* …"For if we have become united with Him in the likeness of His death, certainly we shall also in the likeness of His resurrection; knowing this, that our old self was crucified with Him, that our body of sin might be done away with, that we should no longer be slaves to sin…"Do you not know that when you present yourselves to someone as slaves of obedience, you are slaves of the one whom you obey, either of sin resulting in death, or of obedience resulting in righteousness *(Romans 6:5,6,&16)?*" "You were bought with a price; do not become slaves of men" *(1Corinthians 7:23).*

As I sat there ingesting and digesting God's Word, a lifetime of struggling and yearning became uniquely quieted. I had always believed in God and hungered for His righteousness to be in my life. Now I was coming to see what it takes for that to happen. Quietly and privately, I bowed my head in a deeply heartfelt prayer:

"Father God, thank You for bringing me to see how and why we are enslaved by sin. Thank You for showing me that none of us can free ourselves from it by our own power. Now I realize that You have always understood our human fallenness. We are the ones that need to come to see it, and Your provision for it. Lord, it is awesome to realize that Your love for us is so unselfish, that You willingly clothed Yourself in humanity and came to earth to suffer and die on a cross…in order to pay a debt You knew we could never pay…in order to accomplish a victory and freedom that You knew we would desperately need, but would never be able to attain for ourselves.

"Lord, I am so sorry for all the pain and suffering my sin has cost You. And I gratefully accept the forgiveness You offer me, as I ask and trust You to be my personal Savior and Lord. How could I want anything less, now that I understand how much You love me, and how much I need You. Lord, I have never experienced anyone caring about me that much. Thank You Thank You for giving Your life for me. And thank You for inviting me to give my life to You, Lord Jesus. I ask and trust that as Your Holy Spirit comes to live and reign in me, I will be molded and shaped into becoming the person You want me to be…the person You created me to be….Amen".

"There is therefore now no condemnation
for those who are in Christ Jesus."

Romans 8:1

4

Born Again!

"How wonderful!", I thought…"Jesus Christ living right in and through me as my personal Savior and Lord!" Life was going to be very different now! Goodbye religiosity…hello Christianity! These were some of my thoughts, hopes, and expectations, when for the very first time, I came to understand what salvation by grace really meant.

Although I had been raised to believe in and respect the authority of the Bible, I had never really experienced being taught by it. I had heard years of sermons and a lifetime of admonitions, yet never had I heard such complete explanations. But now, in hearing just exactly what God had to say about my human condition, His Truth had set me free from feelings of guilt and condemnation (John 8:32; Romans 8:1).

Even as a small child I had been aware of Jesus. I had opened my heart to Him, and I had experienced a personal relationship with Him *(Revelations 3:20)*. But now I had come to realize that I wasn't a sinner because I sinned, but that I sinned because I was a born sinner. Now I understood why…"God so loved the world, that He gave His only begotten Son, that whoever believes in Him should not perish, but have eternal life. For God did not send the Son into the world to condemn the world; but that the world might be saved through Him" (John 3:16-17*)*.

Now I had come to better understand the struggle I had always lived with. Now I was able to realize that no matter how hard I tried, my *human* nature didn't have the power to keep God's law. And as I came to realize the power and penalty of sin and that I was no match for its ability to deceive, I felt much more compassion for the plight of Adam and Eve and all the fallen lives that followed theirs, including my own.

I felt so grateful for being offered a freedom from condemnation that I realized I could never have acquired for myself. I was touched… deeply touched by God's Spirit… and I was full of a distinctly new kind of hope.

And now…more than three decades later, how does it all look in retrospect? Was it true? Did the new understanding that I was forgiven and that Jesus had broken sin's power to deceive me, change my life and my circumstances?

Just
Married

5

After The Honeymoon

Well my life certainly changed. Some of the changes were immediate, some were even abrupt. But some of my circumstances didn't seem to change at all, and I battled against them in head, in my heart, and in my prayers. "Why aren't these things changing, Lord?" "What am I doing wrong?"

All through my life I have known people who always seemed to be experiencing victory. They almost seemed like God's preferred persons, like "teachers' pets". They could tell valiant stories of how God sustained them through to victory. They didn't seem to be wrestling with themselves or with their situations. They really seemed above it all. I guess largely because of those examples, I began to believe that being "led by the Spirit", meant being able to be above it all. I thought I was to grow to a place where I would just valiantly trust Jesus in my trials and miraculously I would somehow rise above or be lifted above the feelings of fear, frustration, doubt, anger, and disappointment. I thought that Philippians 4:6&7 suggested that this was what was to happen in times of distress or pain.

"Be anxious for nothing, but in everything by prayer and supplication with thanksgiving let your requests be made known to God…And the peace of God, which surpasses all comprehension, shall guard your hearts and your minds in Christ Jesus."

I thought that if I would just dwell on the positive (Phillip. 4:8), then all the negative feelings would disappear. But I found that even when I would "let my mind dwell on whatever is true, honorable, right, pure, and lovely" all negative feelings did not miraculously disappear. I felt better momentarily perhaps, but when my "positive attitude" wasn't looking, negative feelings would sneak in. And to make matters even worse, guilt plagued me too at those times… guilt for failing to "trust God", failing to just "turn it over to God", failing to just "take God at His Word"…failing to "apply and obey scripture". I just wasn't becoming the tower of strength that I thought I was supposed to become. As a matter of fact, rather than feeling stronger I was feeling weaknesses more and more. Instead of having victories to wave around, I was becoming much more aware of areas of immaturity in my life, and I was realizing how it hurt not only me, but also those around me.

6

Beginning The Process

Then one day, as I was reading God's Word, I came across a scripture verse that seemed to be trying to tell me something very important. I had been drawn more and more too not only read scripture but to study it. I had read Isaiah 66:2…"But to this one I will look…to him who is humble and contrite of spirit, and who trembles at my Word". This verse was much like another verse that had appealed to me: "The sacrifices of God are a broken spirit, a broken and contrite heart O God, Thou wilt not despise" (Psalm 51:17).

I felt moved to look up the key words in these verses and in so doing I found a new kind of comfort. I looked up the word, "humble" and found it to mean, "having or expressing a sense of inferiority, unworthiness or dependence". God was trying to show me my neediness …my need of Him. Next I saw that the word "contrite" meant "broken in spirit because of a sense of sin; penitent; sorry". I realized then that God brings us to a realization of our imperfections, yet saves us from condemnation. Lastly I examined the word "broken", which means "reduced to subjection or incomplete". God was helping me to see how unfinished I was…and that if I submitted myself to Him, He would bring to completion the process He had started in me. He would mold me and shape me into the image bearer that I was designed to be (Philippians 1:6).

Coming to realize, understand, and experience God's tender compassion for my neediness, my imperfection, and my incompleteness was a tremendously healing experience. It gave me a very different sense of personal value and worth that no one…not Satan himself…would ever take away from me.

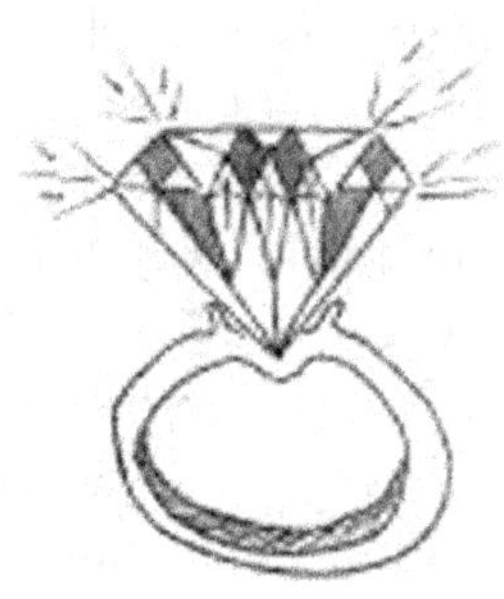

7

Value

Value. What is it? Where does it come from? Webster defines it as…"The worth, merit, usefulness, or importance of something". Much has been recognized about our individual need to feel that we have value. And there is much controversy about how our sense of value or self-esteem is acquired or developed…but perhaps not enough said about how it is lost.

Is self esteem a part of our original design? That is to say, is it a part of our standard equipment like the ability to see or hear? Or is it more like our talents…that need to be recognized in order to be rightly developed?

Perhaps if we look at the original blue print or design of creation, we can come to some determinations.

8

The Value Of The Design

Accoding to the Bible, the original blueprint for the design of humankind was contained in God Himself. "And God created man in His own image, in the image of God He created them; male and female He created them" *(Genesis 1:27)*.

The first chapter of Genesis reports that we are patterned after God and designed to be His image bearers. That means that we can see because He sees, we can hear because He hears, and we can think, do, feel, and relate, because He thinks, does, feels and relates.

Scripture goes on to explain that we are divinely designed to accomplish specific tasks: "And God blessed them ; and God said to them, "Be fruitful, multiply, fill the earth and subdue it"…(Genesis 1:28).

- fruitful (Hebr.parah)…bring forth fruit, growth, and increase
- multiply (Hebr. rebah)…continue, enlarge, gather, and nourish
- replenish (Hebr.mala)…accomplish, furnish, gather, and satisfy
- subdue (Hebr.kabash)…conquer, tame and bring into subjection of *supreme* authority

Thus we see that our ability to produce, reproduce, satisfy, and subdue come as a direct result of being designed to do so. God designed humankind to be able to experience and demonstrate His abilities…to realize, appreciate, and manifest them…in order to actualize them!

This privilege of being a vessel of God's own power and strength is God's gift to us. But as we come to recognize the abilities that have been entrusted to us, we are then in a position to begin to realize the incredible opportunities, as well as the enormous responsibilities, which come with having power and strength!

9

The Potential In Positive Qualities

What qualities do you appreciate the most in a person? Do you like their honesty, or their sensitivity, or maybe their amiability? And what qualities do you most value in yourself?

All positive qualities are positive because they are Divine attributes. They are a part of the character of God. They are parts of God's image that have been entrusted to us. So then why is it that they are not always experienced positively?

Positive qualities don't always feel good because positive qualities can be misused, misunderstood, or misapplied. For instance, loyalty, carried too far, can feel like possessiveness. Enthusiasm can be stretched into fanaticism. Creativity can devolve into day dreaming.

On the following page, you will find a sample of positive qualities that can be experienced negatively. Though this list is certainly neither unique nor exhaustive, it serves to help us realize how it is that a source of potential gain, can become sources of potential pain!

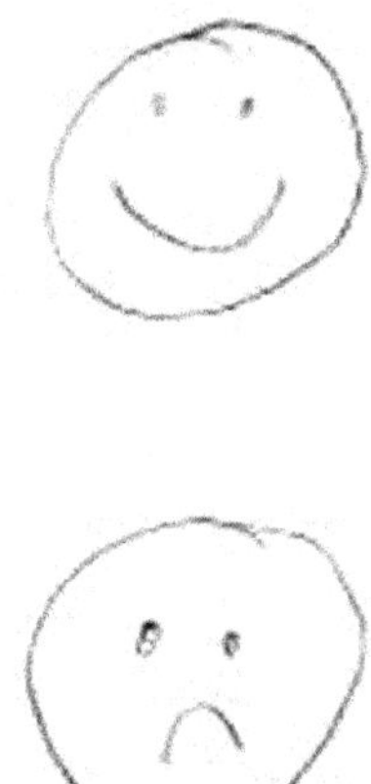

10

Positive Traits Can Be Used Negatively

Influence of the Holy Spirit	Influence of the unholy spirit
1. Amiable; Good Natured	1. Spineless; No Conviction
2. Ambitious; Aspiring	2. Scheming; Pretentious
3. Compassionate; Merciful	3. Gushy; Permissive
4. Confident; Assured	4. Conceited; Overbearing
5. Cooperative	5. Compromising
6. Courageous; Brave	6. Reckless; Brash
7. Courteous; Polite	7. Superficial; Insincere
8. Decisive; Firm	8. Domineering; Inflexible
9. Diligent; Painstaking	9. One Track Mind; Slavish
10. Discerning	10. Critical
11. Efficient; Effective	11. Fussy; Impatient
12. Expressive	12. Talkative; Wordy
13. Flexible	13. Indecisive
14. Forgiving	14. Lenient; Condoning
15. Generous; Liberal	15. Wasteful; Squandering
16. Honest	16. Too Revealing; Blunt
17. Influential; Personable.	17. Manipulative; Seductive
18. Neat; Orderly	18. Over particular
19. Persistent	19. Stubborn
20. Sensitive	20. Touchy

"Do you not know that when you present
yourselves to someone as slaves of obedience,
you are slaves of the one whom you obey,
either of sin resulting in death, or of
obedience resulting in righteousness?"

Romans 6:16

11

Who(se) Are You?

For many years my husband and I hosted various Bible studies in our home. One such study was a family event. Thirteen adults and eleven children met together every Friday night. The adults convened in the family room, while the kids were being supervised in the playroom. After the adults would go over the lesson together, I would slip out of small group discussion time to go downstairs to the playroom to share the main point of that week's study with the children.

One particular week, we were studying the topic of temptation. As I attempted to explain the source of temptation to the children, one young boy named, Joey, seemed especially agitated by what I was saying. Because I had known Joey since he was a baby, he had come to adopt me as his "aunt". And as such, he seemed very free to address the issue very honestly with me. "No, aunt Diane", he insisted, "It's not the devil telling me what to do! Nobody can tell me what to do! I do what *I* want to do! I don't have to listen to the devil, and I don't have to listen to God! I can just listen to me!"

Young Joey's confused sense of independence and personal power gave me the marvelous opportunity to clarify the subject. "Joseph, God has designed us to have what we call a conscience, which is like a little voice inside each one of us", I began to explain. "That means that we are able to recognize the voice of God (good), as well as the voice of not god (evil); And along with the ability to recognize these two differing voices, God has given each of us the ability to choose which one we will listen to or obey. When we choose to follow the voice of God, we become the demonstrator of ***His will***. But when we choose to follow the voice of not god, we become the ***vessel of evil***. 'Me' is the one who gets to decide who's voice I will listen to, repeat, or follow. That is to say that each of us has to decide whether we want to be led by **God's Holy Spirit**…or by the **unholy spirit**".

I went on to try to explain that each of us has been given a free will that allows us to choose whether we want to belong to God or not. And that we need to understand or realize that any time we choose to refuse to be a vessel of God's will…we are automatically Satan's! *(Matthew 12:30)*

12

"Don't Worry…Be Happy!"

In Christian circles we often hear the phrase "salvation by grace." The idea is that we cannot earn our way to heaven, because heaven comes to us by way of faith in Jesus Christ. It is "faith" (taking God at His Word) not "works" (human assessment or effort) that brings us to the opportunity to be saved from sin's doom. Therefore, salvation is said to be a gift, because it is an unmerited favor. It is not something that we have earned. God's Word certainly affirms this to be the case: "For by grace you have been saved through faith; and that not of yourselves, it is the gift of God; not as a result of works, that no one should boast" (Ephesians 2:8&9). So if Jesus died for all our sins, should we ever have to feel guilty for any sin in our lives? After all, we are forgiven and that is all that matters…right?!

It's not hard to understand the universal battle against the feelings of guilt when we realize how much fallenness or sin there is in the world. 1John 5:19 tells us that "the whole world lies in the power of the evil one." Yet 1John 5:18 says, "No one who is born of God sins; but He who was born of God keeps him and the evil one does not touch him". And Hebrews 10:26 says, "For if we go on sinning willfully after receiving the knowledge of the truth, there no longer remains a sacrifice for sins".

So which is it? Am I off the hook concerning this sin thing or not?! After all, nobody's perfect ya know!

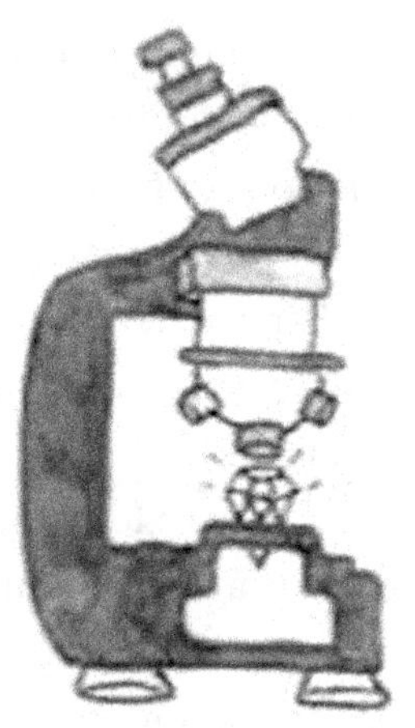

13

Perfection

If you were in the market for diamonds and someone offered you a "great deal" on one, what would you need to know before making the decision to purchase it? Well obviously you would need to know whether the diamond being offered you was worth the asking price. And how could you determine that, unless you knew what it is that gives a diamond its value? And though you may well know that a diamond's value depends on its color, cut, and flawlessness, how good would you be at assessing its condition? Would you know, or know someone who knows, how to accurately recognize and evaluate to what extent its flaws affected its value? Truly flawless diamonds are rare, if existent at all. But the truth is, a diamond doesn't have to be totally perfect to have value. Yet a diamond's value is still determined by how close to perfect it can come.

What is perfection? The dictionary describes it as the state or quality of being perfect; flawlessness; the state of completion or maturity; supreme moral excellence; the highest degree of proficiency. How do you feel about perfection? Is it something you value and want in your life? Or is it something that stirs feelings of irritation or dread?!

"Heaven and earth will pass away, but
My Words will never pass away."

Luke 21:33

14

Expectation

What do you expect out of life? What do you hope to experience, accomplish, or attain? And how or where were those hopes or expectations born?

Our personal anticipations develop from the things we look forward to or expect. But what happens when we look forward to something that never seems to happen, or we expect something we think is due, only to find it absent? Frustration and disappointment are not comfortable feelings. So how can we avoid them…or can we?

All of us started this process called "life" involuntarily. And when we began the process of entering this world, we did so with needs and urges that we had little if any control over. We were dependent. Even before the actual time of our birth, the quality of our existence lay in the hands of others. From our earliest beginnings, "others" had to meet our needs or care for us. Others "fed" us…not only food… but ideas.

It is important for us to realize where our human perceptions or value systems came from. And even more important to recognize to what extent they agree with God's own assessments. Because as each of us move from infancy toward maturity, our perceptions are becoming more accurate…or less accurate.

"He who justifies the wicked and he who condemns the righteous are both alike an abomination to the Lord."

Proverbs 17:15

15

The Development of Conscience

Unfortunately, there may be all too few of us raised in a family where conscience was shaped by God's protective standards. We may not understand healthy guilt (feeling bad for doing bad). Or we may not have ever experienced the relief that comes through healthy confession and repentance (feeling good in turning back to good).

Some of us may have been raised in an environment where sin or fallenness went unrecognized or minimized. The prevailing attitude around us might have been something like, "That's just the way some people are". Behaviors such as irresponsibility, self-centeredness, promiscuity etc. may have gone on unaddressed or accepted uncritically. And such unhealthy toleration of unrighteousness may have seared or damaged the development of a healthy conscience.

Others of us may have been raised in a situation where sin or imperfection was dealt with abusively or unlovingly. We may not have ever seen how fallenness can be respectfully identified and addressed, in order to be openly acknowledged and forgiven. So we may live with a lot of unrelieved guilt. We may often, or even constantly, feel like a failure.

Whether we were raised with attitudes that were very liberal or conservative, each of us has ingested data that has shaped or influenced our individual belief system. In addition to that, we continue to live in a world filled with ever increasing information.

At times we may feel overloaded or even confused by all we see, hear, feel, or think. Some of the values or ideas we are urged to accept are paraded as "new". Others are those that have been handed down to us, perhaps through many generations. Some appear to have the potential of being very valuable. Others have yet to withstand the test of time…

16

How Would You Know?

Imagine having some old pieces of jewelry that belonged to your great grandparents. Picture them tucked away in the back of a dresser drawer. You don't wear any of it because the pieces look too outdated and tarnished. You have been tempted to throw them all out at times. But somehow, because they have been in the family for so many years, it does not seem right to just toss them out. So they have been living in that drawer, pretty much untouched and forgotten. Then one day, while on vacation far from home, you wander into an interesting little antique shop. And while browsing, you happen upon a display case that has some old jewelry pieces in it that look very much like those old pieces you have at home. Fascinated by the coincidence, you inquire about them, explaining that you own some similar pieces.

"Those are very old and very expensive", says the shop-keeper. "You may be the owner of some very valuable pieces and not even realize it!"

So when you get home from your vacation, you dig out the old jewelry pieces and take them to a local antique dealer to have them assessed. Sure enough, you find out that they are very valuable. But you had never enjoyed or benefited from their value because you didn't even know what you had!

How fortunate that you came across someone who could help you recognize and identify the value of the treasure entrusted to you.

"And we also thank God continually because when you received the Word of God, which you heard from us, you accepted it not as the word of men, but as it actually is, the Word of God, which is at work in you who believe."

I Thessalonians 2:13

17

Recognizing Tarnished Treasures

What do you treasure or hold dear? And where do you keep the things you value? How about the things you believe in? Do you tend to wear them publicly? Or are some of them kept tucked away somewhere in the back drawer of your mind, because they seem outdated in today's world? Much like a treasured antique, we sometimes put value on traditions or ideas just because they have "been in the family for years". The merit of some beliefs are not really clear to us. Because as they were passed down from generation to generation, they may have become covered with the tarnish of distortion or misunderstanding. By now they may be so corroded that you are tempted to just get rid of them. But you don't because you keep wondering if in fact there is some real treasure beneath their tarnished exterior. Well perhaps it is time to take a closer look at them in order to assess their real importance.

How much consideration have you given to how your conscience was developed? What influences molded or shaped your sense of value or worth? What circumstances affected you, or continue to affect you and those around you? What beliefs have you inherited… and *whose* ideas are you passing on?

"See to it that no one takes you captive through philosophy and empty deception, according to the traditions of men, according to the elementary principles of the world, rather than according to Christ."

Colossians 2:8

18

Divine Love Defines The Truth

The last six plus decades, I've seen a lot change in what people value. A lot of things have "come and gone", while others seem to have "come full circle". (I guess I should have hung on to some of my old platform shoes, for instance). Then there are those things that seem to have gone from one extreme to another.

For instance, while growing up, the terms "hell, fire, and damnation" were pretty popular. Now, however, the sentiment seems to have shifted to the opposite extreme…love, love, and love! Our current society, being used to much gratification, seems very uncomfortable with the idea of "consequences". So perhaps in an attempt to approach God, life, or one another more positively, we may hear an emphasis on love at the expense of truth. But Truth and Love are inherent attributes of God. They function in conjunction with one another like two sides of the same coin. Therefore, they can not be separated without distorting both.

God is Love (1John 4:7-8). But God is also Truth (John 14:6). They are designed to function in Holy Union. Because, *Love without Truth manipulates.* And *Truth without Love intimidates. But God's Truth, exposed in an atmosphere of God's Love, liberates!*

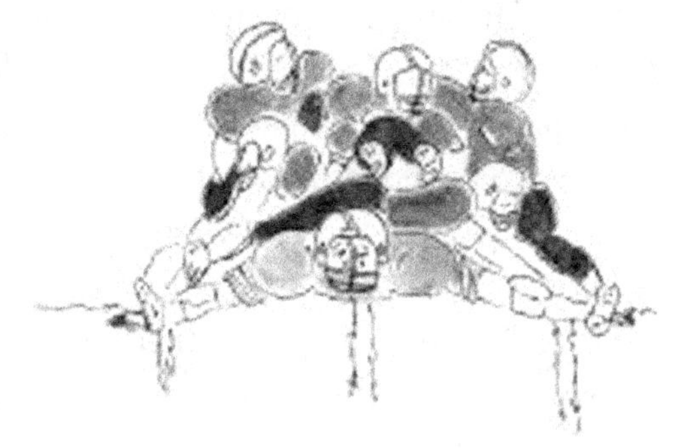

19

Becoming Liberated

All along the road of my life I have seen people reaching or struggling to "get", "have", or "be". They labor to identify and develop their potential, so that they can possess the things they value. Such a quest can certainly be motivated by a healthy desire for self-discovery, the desire to become all we can be. But, regrettably, selfishness or greed can also motivate it. History records many a battle fought because those with power yearned for "more", while those without power yearned for "some". Power was assessed to be the biggest prize, therefore, vying for power became the biggest battle.

To feel powerless is to feel a lack of control over our own fate. So feeling powerless leads us to feelings of fear. As a result, we desire freedom from that fear, and the acquiring of power seems like the best method of attaining freedom. But what does power actually bring? Is not the person in the precarious possession of power in a similar position as a football player in a lively football game…in that every time the player is in possession of the ball… everybody is aiming for him or running him down?

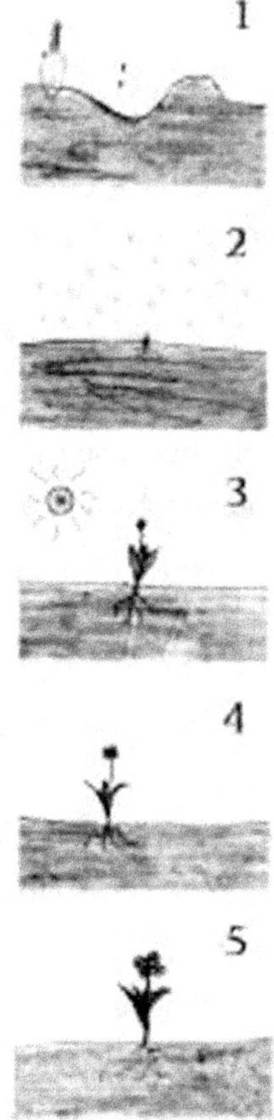

1
2
3
4
5

20

The Truth About Wimps!

Because I often felt like one, I remember asking the Lord how He felt about wimps. One day, during the privacy of my early morning jog, I dared to ask…

"Lord, do You love wimps? Is it only the strong and courageous like King David or the Apostle Paul that please you? I feel like a looser, Lord…I don't have any big, bold victories to impress You with…I feel like a wimp, Lord! Can You love a wimp?"

"A wimp is just a limp hope not yet born", I thought I heard Him say. "All unborn hopes and dreams start out as lifeless wimps." Then His Word coursed through me. "Truly, truly, I say to you that unless a grain of wheat falls into the earth and dies, it remains by itself alone…But if it dies, it bears much fruit" (John 12:24). "That which you sow does not come to life unless it dies" (1Corinthians 15:36).

I felt God bringing me to see that lifelessness is His starting point. God is in the business of breathing life into wimps…limp hopes…and bearing fruit through them. Unborn victories will never come alive apart from God breathing His life into them. Feeling like a wimp is a marvelous first step in recognizing our own helplessness, and thus our need for God working in us!

"He who is not with Me is against Me; and he who does not gather with Me scatters."

Matthew 12:30

21

True Christianity

Only in true Christianity can we find real hope. Because only there are we given to understand the depth of our own need for God. God's Word declares that man is a born sinner and unable to save himself from the enslaving power of sin. But God's Word also explains that Jesus, The Christ, The Word in the flesh…is the provided Savior of mankind (Isaiah 45:18-25; John 15:4-6). Only Christians (Christ ones) proclaim Jesus to be both God and man…having been born of a Divine Father and a human mother…creating a Holy Union of God's Divine Spirit and God designed flesh (Isaiah 9:6-7; Matthew 1:18-25; 1John 4:9-10). True believers understand that God sent His Own flesh and blood, Jesus, God with skin on, to be the mediator between God and man (Timothy 2:3-5).

Yet, history records that when Jesus came claiming to be the Son of God, One with God…they crucified Him (John 10:30; Luke 23). They didn't believe Jesus was, in fact, their predicted Messiah, because they expected their Messiah to be a person of earthly power and influence…not one of divine humility and sacrifice (John 1:11). Though their Torah contained over 300 references to the coming of their Messiah, they didn't recognize Him when He came because they were basing their faith on what seemed logical to them. And what Jesus was saying to them sounded unreasonable. His Words made no sense to their humanistic minds and hearts. So they trusted human reasoning…instead of Divine Revelation (1 Corinthians 2: 12-14).

Today Christians base their faith on God's Word, the Bible. Yet how many really know the difference between the God of the Bible, and the God designed by human reason. How many wouldn't recognize Jesus Christ even if He was right in their midst…because they are hanging on to some very humanistic concepts of Him… rather than taking Him at His Word?

22

Judgement

It has been very interesting to me to notice that often it is people who have little if anything to do with the bible, that love to quote one particular verse; "Do not judge lest you be judged yourselves" *(Matthew 7:1)*. Apparently those that seek to use that verse to justify or minimize sin, think that if they ignore everyone else's sin, God will ignore theirs. Is that true? Is that the system that God is seeking to bring to us?

Imagine, if you will for a moment, what would happen if the whole world decided to live by any standard they deemed appropriate or advantageous at the moment? What would happen if "each man did what was right in their own eyes" *(Judges 17:6)?* The answer to that question is seen in our world's history as it evidences again and again that…"There is a way, which seems right to a man, but its end is the way of death" *(Proverbs 14:12)*. Yet we can benefit from the mistakes of the past as they give us the opportunity to realize that…"Wisdom rests in the heart of one who has understanding, but in the bosom of fools it is made known"*(Proverbs 14:33)*. Here we are given to see that being wise requires that we have understanding of God's Will, while being a fool asks only that we lack or disregard His good judgement. Only God's judgements are totally accurate. Only His assessments will continue to be proven true. So when we comply with His Word, we are proving that we believe and value His "Protective Directives". But if we disregard or deviate from His Word, we are demonstrating the poor judgement of a fool.

23

"Pretending"

One of the favorite games of my childhood was a game we all called "dress up". My friends and I solicited old clothes from anywhere we could. We gathered grownup's old skirts, shirts, pants, coats, dresses, shoes, hats, gloves, and jewelry. We used props of all kinds. Even things like old curtains proved useful to our creative little minds. After we collected everything, we then had to decide who would get to wear what. With the girls, there was often a favored pair of "high heels" that became the desired trophy...with the boys, any "dad's boots". We had so much fun dressing up in those "grown up clothes"! And, of course, we had to make up little living stories or plays to go along with our adventures in "pretend". Our attempts to be grown up were naturally modeled after the adults around us. We tried to act like we had seen them act. We tried to "walk in their shoes". We sought to stride in confidence and grace as we wobbled place to place. We thought we looked great! And as we paraded ourselves in front of every adult we could find, we thought our perceptions about ourselves were being affirmed... as they all gave us great big smiles!

Because the game of "pretend" was so much fun, we didn't have a clue that the image we sought to wear, fit us about as well as the "old dress up clothes" did.

24

Growing Into (Or Out Of) Our Clothes

Like the process of growth itself, that old game we called "dress up" seems to be ageless. My childhood friends and I enjoyed it…my children and their friends enjoyed it…and I enjoyed watching my grandchildren and their friends experience it. Perhaps the appeal of that old game lies in our desire to reach out for the "next step" in life. Pretending, reaching out, trying, including trying on images that we hope to attain, are all a familiar part of growing up.

As my mind's eye remembered and thought about the precious picture of children dressed up in "grown up clothes", I thought of how we must look when we try to wear the image of God, an image that is understandably way to big for us, and yet one that we have been designed to grow into. And I thought of how God must view us when He sees us parading around various characteristics that are obviously still so big on us that we're tripping on them…or…how He feels about the ones that are clearly too small for us.

When God created you and me, He knew just what it was going to take to bring us from inception to birth, infancy to maturity. We were born naked and helpless. But as we grew, we struggled to learn how to do things for ourselves in an attempt to establish a sense of our competency. Among other things, we learned to put on and eventually even choose our own clothes. Those clothes often represented "images" that we sought to wear, to give us a sense of our own personal identity. Some demonstrated a desire to "fit in", while others revealed a desire to "stand out". Perhaps a good question to ask is what is it we wanted to fit into…and what were we trying to stand out or away from?

In our society there is a lot of emphasis on having the right "look" or creating a particular "image". Human nature seems easily influenced by those who "supposedly know" what is or is not "fashionable" at the moment. But just who is it that is seeking to lead us into the habit of wearing whatever is fashionable at the moment? What is the motive behind the pressure to buy whatever they are selling? Why do they care what we wear…or how we look? Are they seeking what is profitable for us…or what is profitable for them?

Well there is someone else who cares what we wear, or how we look. He is the One who created beauty and style. He cares very much what our "coverings" may cost us…because He, more than anyone else, understands our need of value and protection. That's why He offers to lead us…to what will clothe us in beauty and benefit… forever!

Section III

Do You *Know* What You Need?

1

Can You Help Me?

It was cold and getting dark, and I knew I needed to get from where I was, to a place of warmth and safety. So I tried to hail down the big bus I saw coming down the street that I was walking along. But as the huge vehicle approached, it seemed oblivious to my waving arms and verbal pleas. So as it passed me by, I thought to myself, "It must be that the bus will only stop at certain places along its designated route". So I kept walking along the edge of the road, expecting that sooner or later I would come to one. And then, finally, there it was! I could see it up ahead! Tired, yet anxious, I tried to run to it as I realized another bus was on the horizon. Surely, this time the bus would respond to my obvious need! And sure enough, the bus began to slow down as it approached. As it rolled to a stop, relieved, I stumbled toward its closed doors. In response to my knocking, the folded doors began to part. My out-stretched leg reached for the bottom step. But the first step seemed so steep, that I could barely reach it. So I grasped onto the side rails with both hands and literally pulled myself up.

"I made it…thank God I made it", I thought appreciatively. But as my eyes sought those of the bus driver, in the desire to express my thanks, confusion and fear gripped me when I found myself staring into the barrel of his gun. And as he extended his right hand directly at me, he shot me point blank in my forehead. The force of the bullet propelled me from the steps of the bus into a drainage ditch along side the road. The next sound I heard was the sound of the bus driving away.

My mind reeled in a desperate struggle to understand! What had just happened??…And why? Why?! Why??!! What had I done to bring this about!? Was I dead already? Or was I dying? The thought that maybe I was daydreaming the whole thing came to mind. So I decided to reach up and touch my forehead to see if anything was really there. My arms felt like they were too heavy to be able to move. But as I slowly drew one hand to my head, my index finger slid into the hole discovered there. And as my body became aware that it was lying in a pool of liquid, I can remember the feel and smell of what seemed to me to be wet grass. "Oh God, oh God, what is going on?", I kept asking. And then God answered my prayer…by awakening me from the frightful nightmare that He had allowed me to dream. But while waking up relieved my immediate fear, dreaming the dream awakened me to an awareness of some very difficult questions that required learning about some very awesome Divine answers.

"I will say of the Lord, He is my refuge and
my fortress, my God, in whom I trust."

"He will cover you with His feathers, and
under His wings you will find refuge; His
faithfulness will be your shield and rampart."

Psalms 91:2 & 4

2

Looking for Solid Ground

"All I have is you, Lord! You are the only One standing between despair and me." Have you ever heard yourself saying these words or something similar? Hard truths are potential hope killers. Therefore, when we're faced with them, we may try several methods to escape them. We can try to just shut them out, or reshape them in our minds to make them more tolerable. We might minimize, rationalize, justify, or even retaliate. But all of these methods are killers of hope, killers of faith, and killers of discovery.

God knows and understands how much we struggle in our desire to understand how to deal with some of the really difficult experiences that find their way into our lives. Therefore, He continually encourages us and coaches us to personally address the truths that He knows will bring us to new realizations of freedom and victory. Personally, I think the hardest thing for me to face was my own sense of helplessness… because I had spent so many years trying to overcome it!

In the Bible, the 6th chapter of John shows Jesus' followers struggling against some hard realities that Jesus was seeking to help them face. Few were willing to allow these deeper truths into their mind. As a result, "Many of His followers withdrew and were not walking with Him anymore." Jesus therefore said to the twelve disciples, "You do not want to leave too, do you?" Simon Peter answered, "Lord, to whom shall we go?" The disciples had come to know what we need to remember; that turning away from God means turning away from the only One who has the real answer (John 6:66, 67, 68).

3

Common Dilemmas

Human nature is complex, yet our human natures have a lot in common. How we wish these commonalties were all positive; we like to share in the good times. So why is it then, that stories about good times don't sell nearly as well as stories about human struggles?

Book after book, program after program, film after film… human nature is seen yearning and struggling for something. The struggling leads to convening, deceiving, giving, taking, winning, loosing, leaving and returning. All these stories are reaching their targeted audiences because people can relate to each scene; as a piece of themselves is being identified or revealed…or even released…from its secret place of careful confinement.

Young, old, or anywhere in between, yearning and suffering can touch you where you live. It doesn't even have to be your own suffering in order to affect you deeply. The sight of it or the mere realization of its existence can promote emotional responses such as dread or fear. So while we watch, we do so with the hope of a good ending. We want to see dread and fear overcome, because we are not necessarily comfortable with the reality of our own weaknesses.

"For it is better, if God should will it so, that you suffer for what is right rather than for doing what is wrong".

1 Peter 3:17

4

The Pain Of Weakness

What's so bad about weakness? Well, weakness makes us feel vulnerable; it proves that we're not all powerful. And if we are not all powerful, how can we protect ourselves…from whatever it is we do not want, like pain, or deprivation?

Frankly, I don't remember volunteering for either miserable state. Yet both have found their way into my life many times, in spite of my best efforts to stop them. But some of the discomfort of pain and deprivation came from a misconception that I had. You see, I tended to equate discomfort with punishment, instead of realizing that it can also be the evidence of healthy resistance to evil. And I also tended to equate the lack of discomfort with reward, instead of understanding that it can also be the evidence of refusing to resist the invasive efforts of evil.

God's gracious correction of my misunderstanding can be seen through the pages of a personal journal that I was writing during a particularly difficult time of pain in my life.

"Lord, is this the 'payoff' of obedience?", I asked. I hadn't expected a trophy or even recognition necessarily. But I hadn't expected the "let down" that I was experiencing either. What had I done wrong? Why was my obedience bringing such negative consequences? It didn't seem fair to have to suffer so for doing the right thing! I guess I was expecting some breakthrough, some blessing. But instead, things seemed to be getting even worse. "Obedience costs too much, Lord!", I cried.

The Lord's answer to me was as profound as it was timely. "But remember", He suggested, "the ultimate source of all pain is 'evil' and freedom from all pain will ultimately come through 'righteousness'... so which do you want to continue to choose"?

It was then I realized that in this world of "free will" we all have to face the pain of resisting evil...or else succumb to the pain of allowing it to prevail. Evil will never retreat voluntarily...because like a cancer, it is sustained by capturing and consuming healthy or "good" cells!

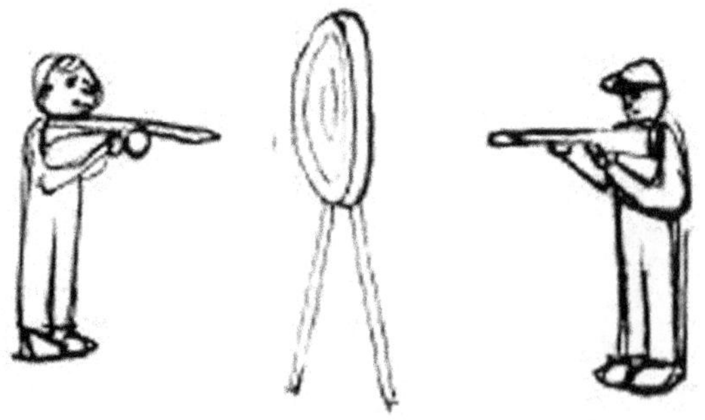

5

Competition

Just how good is "good"? And what does it take to answer that question? How do we know if or when "good" is good enough? Today, competitive opposition is as popular as it is prevalent in our culture. Competition invites us to expose what we've got in comparison to what someone else has, in an attempt to prove who or what is better. Competition tests our competence as it exposes our comparative fitness. But perhaps competition has an even higher purpose. Perhaps its greater value is in its ability to instruct us as to what is possible under a given set of circumstances.

When it comes to the competition between good and evil, God Himself assumed the responsibility for proving which is greater or ultimately victorious. But superior as righteousness is, God knows we also need to realize how it is that under certain conditions, the experience of its value may become lost.

"Blessed are those who hunger and thirst
for righteousness, for they will be filled".

Matthew 5:6

6

Understanding Human Longings

As we look at the history of mankind, we are given to see a very specific and common denominator – man's longing. All throughout history, mankind is seen longing… longing for satisfaction…longing for freedom…longing for (you fill in the blank).

Where does the "longing" inside us come from? What will satisfy it? Plenty of differing opinions attempt to answer that question. But until we understand what that inner yearning is, and why we have it, we won't know what to do with it.

Our capacity to experience gratification is a gift to us from God. Made in God's image, we have this capacity because He does. But God, our Creator and Designer, is the only one who knows just how and when our desire for gratification must be satisfied, and how and when it must be restrained in order for us to be protected. Unfortunately however, the naiveté of human nature tends to assume that it automatically knows how to handle "desire". And it tends to *equate "freedom" with the absence of limitation…not realizing that the absence of limits or restraint is what kills, robs, and destroys the beauty of gratification.* Without the ability to subdue or limit our desire for gratification, we will cross the line of its original design, and there by bring pain instead of gain. Thus we will come to destroy…that which was designed to protectively nourish and satisfy.

"Greater love has no one than this, that
he lay down his life for His friends".

John 15:13

7

The Beauty of Power

Can you imagine where we would all be if God Himself wasn't able to restrain or control His power, His urges, and His desire to be gratified?! In giving much thought to that question, I have come to believe that God's most incredible power is His ability to *withhold* His power. I am in awe of His willingness to choose to suffer in order to provide for and protect what is precious to Him…US!

Why are we precious to God? Why does He even care about what we do? After all, He's the One with all the power, so how can we pose any kind of threat to Him? Why does He not take full advantage of His power over us by simply forcing us or manipulating us into gratifying Him? Or why did He not create us to just automatically gratify any or all of His desires? Well, maybe we can answer those questions by asking ourselves some others.

What power is greater than the power to take gratification unto ourselves, any time and anyway we want to? What has the power to motivate us to withhold our power, or to use our power for the sake of another? What moves us to want to share what we have, instead of just hoarding it all to ourselves? And what in the world is powerful enough to bring us to the place where we are even willing to suffer if need be, for the sake of another?

"Abide in Me, and I in you. As the branch can not bear fruit of itself, unless it abides in the vine, so neither can you, unless you abide in Me".

John 15:4

8

The Road To Satisfaction

Our bodies have been designed by God to be able to host the experience or sensation of pleasure. But that pleasure or satisfaction originates in our spirit, and is brought to our body through the avenue of our mind. We can diligently seek to gratify the physical body, but unless the mind and spirit are functionally able to process that gratification, the body won't be able to experience the desired satisfaction. For example, a depressed person may want very much and try very hard to experience satisfaction, yet find themself unable to. Because their mind needs to become freed up or empowered to receive and transmit the message from the spirit to the body. So what is it that has the power to interfere with that Divinely Designed process? And who or what can remove such interference?

Pleasure was God's idea. He is the One who introduced us to it in the first place. Only He knows just exactly when and how we are to experience it. And only He knows just exactly when and how it becomes maligned. But there are those who are trying to assert that man, not God, is the one to decide pleasure's limits or lack of limits. They see themselves as powerful enough to attain gratification through their own efforts. They perceive themselves shrewd enough to enjoy God's given pleasures without the seeming interference of God's designed limits. But their perceptions are full of deceptions. They are people with an incomplete understanding of God, as well as incomplete understanding of the danger and destructiveness of their own vulnerable humanness. They don't understand who created them and why. And they don't understand true satisfaction, because they have only tasted its temporary counterfeit. If they were to meet someone who said they had it, how would they know whether what that other person had, was any better than what they themselves had? God's Word teaches what Christ's true followers, through obedience, come to know. Which is, that God's avenue of true or ultimate gratification is in contradiction to human understanding. That's why man will never find it by himself (1Corinthians 2:7-16).

Sin, which is any deviation from God's design, damages pleasure. Sin, which is any resistance to the leading of God's Holy Spirit, interferes with our being able to receive the experience of God's designed best.

"There is a way which seemeth right unto a man,
but the end thereof are the ways of death."

Proverbs 14:12

9

Appreciating the Value of Limits

Our society seems to have little problem with the concept of laws or rules when it comes to sports. All sports have set boundaries for what is and is not acceptable behavior. We are also familiar with and accepting of rules when it comes to playing games, like Monopoly or Checkers. In determining rules and regulations for various sports or games, man is deciding how the game is to be played…and what it will take to win.

There are other laws that our society accepts, even though we did not have anything to do with establishing them. We call them natural laws, like the law of gravity. We learn to live with them—we even learn to make good use of them—because we know that we can not just defy them without consequence.

Then there are laws that man attempts to establish within a society, so that we don't take unfair advantage of one another. Laws are what prohibit us from misusing our free will. Laws are what warn us away from harm.

When man establishes a law, he is determining what *he* thinks should or should not happen. But when God identifies **His** law, He is proclaiming truth. He is warning us of what is. And what **He** declares to be true **is** true, whether we know it and whether we believe it or not. God's laws are for us not against us. His protective directives are to teach us how to utilize all the marvelous gifts and abilities that He created us to have. He knows we need to realize that all we have been given, including our free will, can become detrimental… if improperly used!

"... Faith cometh by hearing, and
hearing by the word of God".

Romans 10:17

"All Scripture is inspired by God and
profitable for teaching, for reproof, for
correction, and training in righteousness".

2 Timothy 3:16

"Study to show thyself approved unto God,
a workman that needeth not to be ashamed,
rightly dividing the Word of Truth".

2 Timothy 2:15

10

Faith Comes by Hearing the Word

Most of us don't get up in the morning thinking, "I think I'll do something stupid and hurtful today". Yet we do sometimes make "mistakes" that in retrospect, we realize were foolish. Why? Because we tend to make choices based on what we know, or what we think we know.

In Acts 18:25-26 we learn of a man named Apollos who believed in God, but was incomplete in his understanding of Him. The Scriptures describes him as being "fervent in spirit", therefore he was boldly speaking and teaching from what he knew. As he did this, two other more mature believers, Priscilla and Aquila, in recognizing his lack of information, "took him aside and explained to him the way of God more accurately". In Acts 19:1-10, we see a similar example of the need for our faith (what we believe) to become schooled by truth because truth is what safeguards us from the consequences of error.

God's Holy Spirit of Truth is released to us through redemption. When Jesus, God with skin on, came to this earth, He exposed human error, and offered an options to it. He offered to guide man's thinking, by offering him something more than just human reasoning. Because He knew we needed something more. He knew we needed to be guided by His Divine understanding. But this protective process can only become actualized in us through our entrusting ourselves to…committing ourselves to…relying on or believing in…Jesus, the Living Word of Truth.

In Luke 3:3-17 we see John the Baptist very angry with a group of people who were claiming to be "saved". The bases of their claim was that they were "Jews", "children of Abraham", and therefore children of God by lineage. These men did believe in the existence of God, but they did not have an accurate understanding of how to acquire salvation…that is, freedom from sin's compulsion and consequence. So they were claiming to have something that their attitudes, motivations and behaviors very much contradicted.

"You will know them by their fruits. Grapes are not gathered from thornbushes, nor figs from thistles, are they? So then, you will know them by their fruits. Not everyone who says to Me, 'Lord, Lord', will enter the kingdom of heaven; but he who does the will of My Father who is heaven" (Matthew 7:16, 20, 21).

"Why do you call me 'Lord, Lord,' and do not do what I say" (Luke 6:46)? "My sheep hear my voice, and I know them, and they follow Me; and I give eternal life to them, and they shall never perish; and no one shall snatch them out of My hand "(John 10:27).

So where do you want to live? In the palm of God's hand…or out on your own?

11

Knowing Our Limits

Someone offends or irritates us and we try to be patient with them. Still, we "lose it", in spite of our best efforts not to! Or, maybe our struggle is to lose a few pounds (or maybe more than just a few), and we become determined to stay on a diet. We really do try, but we find ourselves thinking, "I can't…I just can't do it!"

Some believe that it is God's voice that is saying to them…"Yes you can…just try a little harder!"…Or…"You have to…You just have to put your mind to it and do it because it has to be done!" But such a voice is not God's. Commanding as God's voice is, it does not "demand". God understands better than we do what our "human" limits are, and what *empowerment* we need to do the task we have been called to.

I can remember trying to find my car keys one day. I had taken them off the key rack by the front door on my way out to my car. Then, realizing that I had forgotten something, I headed back into the house to get it. In the process, I set my keys down…someplace! As I searched for them I kept soliciting the Lord's help. This particular day my pleas seemed to go unheard and time was ticking away. Threatened by the prospect of being late for my appointment, I began to feel more and more frustrated. Finally, in desperation, I remember saying, "Lord, I can't locate those keys one second before you lead my eyes to see them, or my mind to where to look for them!" At that moment my eyes fell on the keys sitting on the bathroom sink. I gratefully thanked the Lord and went on my way. But my words have come back to mind many times since… "Lord, I can't locate those keys one second before you lead my eyes to see them, or my mind to where to look!"

"…apart from Me you can do nothing".

John 15:5

12

Unrealistic Expectations

How often do we find ourselves trying to live up to an expectation that is impossible at the moment? And how many times have we put unrealistic expectations on others? How about that absurd question often heard from the lips an exasperated parent, "Why don't you grow up!"...Or that famous directive toward a toddler, "Sit still!" How about the line we can hate hearing when we are upset about something very important to us, "Just don't let it bother you!"... or..."You shouldn't feel that way!"

Often we wish we did have a control button to change the channel of our energies. If only it was that easy. Some would indicate that we do have such a control button, insisting that it is simply a matter of will power..."mind over matter"!

What do we think God has to say to us at such times? Do we picture Him pulling us by the arm...or pushing us from behind? Do we imagine Him to be disgusted with us when we feel like we "just can't"?

Where do we get our ideas and expectations about God, others, and ourselves? Just how accurate are they? Can we make the impossible happen, just by trying hard enough or believing strongly enough?

When we are not quite sure what to believe or expect, I think we are apt to look to others who seem sure of themselves or to someone we know is sincere. We crave affirmation. But affirmation comes by way of information. Because by definition the word, affirmation, means…"The act of affirming or asserting as true". So only as we come to know what is true…what the "Ultimate Authority" says is true about us and our situation…can we come to the experience of true encouragement and security…through a reassuring confirmation of our value…as well as an appropriate provision for our circumstances.

"He who rejects Me, and does not receive
My sayings, has one who judges him; the word
I spoke is what will judge him at the last day."

John 12:48

13

The Validity and Value of the Bible

When God created us, He also created a tangible means of learning from Him. He did not just plop us here on earth with no instructions or road map. Starting with Adam and Eve, God's provision of guidance came through the avenue of His Words. He offered protective directives from the very beginning, thereby providing an option to learning everything the hard way.

In and of itself, doing things the hard way is not the most effective way to learn. Because while struggling can indicate to us that something is difficult, it does not automatically lead us to realize whether or not it is profitable. Hence, the old saying, "If all else fails, read the directions."

God offers direction, insight, and understanding through His word, the Bible. About 40 different men wrote the Bible over a period of some 1600 years. The writings date from about 1500 years before Christ, to about 100 years after His death. And though these authors did not all know one another, or even all live at the same time, their writings affirmed one another, evidencing the inspiration of the same, One and Only, Holy Spirit. The reason the Bible is so critical to our faith is because it makes claims and predictions that, one-by-one, prove to be true. The Truth of God's Word is what shines the light of dawn on the world of darkness. God's Word is what exposes the existence of the ignorance and error that come with the territory of **human false assumption.**

14

Words = Tangible Expression

Where in the world would we be without words… thought words, written words, spoken words? Words communicate…words express…words make tangible or understandable, what would otherwise remain unknown!

In the first Chapter of Genesis we read that God *spoke* the world into existence. He converted what was in His Mind into tangible form, through the avenue of words! "Then God said, 'Let there be light", and there was light' (vs.3). "Then God said, 'Let there be an expanse in the midst of the waters, and let it separate the waters from the waters' (vs. 6). "Then God said, 'Let the waters below the heavens be gathered into one place, and let dry land appear' (vs.9). "Then God said, 'Let the earth sprout vegetation, plants yielding seed, and fruit trees bearing fruit after their kind, with seed in them, on the earth' (vs.11). "Then God said, 'Let there be lights in the expanse of the heavens to separate the day from the night, and let them be for signs, and for seasons, and for days and years; and let them be for lights in the expanse of the heavens to give light on the earth' (vs. 14&15). "Then God said, 'Let the waters teem with swarms of living creatures, and let birds fly above the earth in the open expanse of the heavens' (vs. 20). "Then God said, 'Let the earth bring forth living creatures after their kind: cattle and creeping things and beasts of the earth after their kind'…(vs. 24). ***Then God said*** *…"Then God said"…and it was so!*

Here in these verses, and in all of Scripture, we see a mysterious and marvelous power at work. We see God choosing specifically descriptive, carefully selected… words…to give identity to His wonderfully diversified and unique creation. We see God choosing to reveal and explain Himself…through His Word!

"In the beginning was the Word, and the
Word was with God, and the Word was God."

John 1:1

15

Revelation

Words are a vehicle that can be used to reveal the existence of the Divine. God knows that what is "spiritual" needs to be described or demonstrated so it can be recognized or understood.

John 1:1 explains that "The Word" existed "from the beginning" and is a manifestation of God. Identifying Himself first through the vehicle of verbal expression, God then began revealing Himself through the avenue of visible creation. And as God's Own Unique Image was designed into His creation of mankind, His Own Uniquely Powerful Abilities were there by given an avenue of display. As "The Word" was made tangible, life became perceptible. Thus, we were enabled to recognize and appreciate the awesome reality of God.

Then, in an expression of God's Highest Good, Jesus the Christ, God with skin on, came to show humanity what His Highest Good (Holiness or Wholeness) looks like when it is "lived out" in human form. Jesus, God's own flesh and blood, demonstrated how righteousness thinks, how it acts, and what it lives for. Through the life, death, and resurrection of Jesus, we are given the opportunity to realize the beauty and benefit of God's Truth and God's Love…as well as the destruction and loss that exist in their absence.

"...It is written, 'Man shall not live by bread alone, but on every word that proceeds out of the mouth of God".

Matthew 4:4

16

The Word

In the beginning was the Word, and the Word was with God, and the Word was God…He was in the beginning with God. All things came into being through Him; apart from Him nothing came into being that has come into being…"And the Word became flesh, and dwelt among us, and we beheld His glory, glory as of the only begotten from the Father, full of grace *(grace-gr. charis: the Divine influence upon the heart, and its reflection in the life)…*and truth *(truth-gr. alethlia: true and vital reality* (John 1:1-3 and 14).

"In Him was life; and the life was the light of men; And the light shineth in the darkness; and the darkness did not comprehend it…"He was in the world, and the world was made through Him, and the world did not know Him…He came to His own, and those who were His own did not receive Him…But as many as received Him, to them He gave the *right to become* children of God, even to those who believe in His *name (Gr. onoma: authority, character)…* who were born not of blood, nor of the will of the flesh, nor of the will of man, but of God" (John 1:4-5 and 10-13).

"For God so loved the world, that He gave His only begotten Son, that whoever believes *(believes-gr. pisteuo: entrust one's self to; commit to)* in Him should not perish, but have eternal life. For God did not send the Son into the world to condemn the world; but that the world should be saved through Him" (John 3:16-17). "I have come as light into the world, that everyone who believes in me may not remain in darkness. And if any one hears My sayings, and does not keep them, I do not condemn him for I did not come to sentence the world to damnation, but to save the world. He who rejects Me, and does not receive My sayings, has one who condemns him; the Word I spoke is what will judge him at the last day" (John 12:46-48).

"My sheep hear my voice, and I know them, and they follow me".

John 10:27

17

A Wake-Up Call...

Have you ever been sound asleep in a dark room...and then, had someone come into that room and turn on the light in order to wake you up? What was your first reaction? Was it to quickly cover your eyes, perhaps, in order to protect them from the pain of having them subjected to sudden bright light after they had become used to the comfort of darkness? That is exactly what used to happen when my dad used that method to wake up my sisters and me when we were little.

I can still hear the sounds of my dad getting up before dawn on cold winter mornings and going to the basement to stoke the coal furnace so our family could wake up to a warm house. After he got the embers of the night's fire rekindled, he would come upstairs to the bedroom that my sisters and I shared...and wake us up in time for school. He would do this by flipping our ceiling light on and off a few times while announcing, "It's time to get up, girls"!

As I thought about the process of learning that we all go through, I saw how sometimes what God is seeking to show us feels like the sudden brightness of the light in my bedroom...like an unwelcome intrusion, a disruption to my comfort. My dad tried to be merciful by flicking the light on and off a few times, in an attempt to help us get used to the brightness of the light. But even as he did, we would sometimes pull the covers over our head in an attempt to avoid the inevitable. Yet, even as we did, we knew we were being "called" to let go of our slumber.

But, you know an interesting thing happened. One morning, as my dad returned from his dutiful trip to the coal stove in the basement, and proceeded to our bedroom to get us up…as he reached in and flipped our light switch…no light came on because the light bulb had burned out. But even though the light did not go on, just the sound of the light switch being flipped was enough to alert us to his wake-up call. And so for the next few days, though the ceiling light had yet to be replaced, my dad continued his early morning ritual. And each morning, at the mere *sound* of the switch, my sisters and I instinctively understood and automatically responded to the call to get up. Because ***my father had trained us to instinctively recognize his message!***

"Again Jesus therefore spoke to them, saying, 'I Am the Light of the world; he who follows Me shall not walk in darkness...

John 8:12

18

Light

If you look up the word "light" in the dictionary, you will find some pretty lengthy descriptions such as:

- ❏ An illuminating agent or source
- ❏ A form of radiant energy
- ❏ Mental or spiritual illumination
- ❏ To become aware of or understand
- ❏ Easy to endure, deal with, or perform
- ❏ Free from sorrow or care
- ❏ To come to rest or settle down on something

In John 8:12 Jesus describes Himself as "the light of the world", and reassures us that "he who follows Me shall not walk in darkness, but shall have the light of life."

When Jesus came to this earth, He came with a specific task or purpose; He came to free us from darkness. He came as the "illuminating energy source" or "food of life". He came to bring us to "see" what only He can show us. He came to rouse our eyes from slumber, by training our ears to hear Him!

19

Distinguishing Between Good & Evil

What color eyes does goodness have? What size shoe does evil wear? These might seem like silly questions…but they introduce a very important issue.

"Good" and "bad" are only abstract ideas…until we are able to "see" them in some kind of practical or applied tangible form. So if the "spirit of goodness" was floating around somewhere, what good would it do? What benefit would be realized from it? And for that matter, if the "spirit of evil" was lurking among us, what harm could it accomplish? Do not good and evil need an avenue of expression or an available vessel in order to be recognized or experienced?

When a baby is born, (or even before), how does he or she come to decide what is good and what is not? What does it take to discover and evaluate all of the incredible possibilities that come with the territory of humanness? For instance, how does an infant come to the realization that the fingers on the end of his hand belong to him… and that they can move in marvelous ways…like reaching for and grasping desired objects of fascination?

Discovering and developing our potential takes some intense effort on our part…at least at first…until we get the hang of it! But as we come to experience the sense of power and fulfillment that come with accomplishment, we begin to realize that we possess a power that can be directed to accomplish something positive and beneficial, or something negative and destructive. We can become an expressive avenue of goodness, or a powerful vehicle of evil.

20

Peace By Piece

In the biblical account of Creation (Genesis 1&2), we see a very detailed description of a step-by-step, piece-by-piece process. And here we are given to see that while every aspect of creation was divinely designed with a specific purpose, it was also designed to "function in conjunction". That is to say, each piece of creation is only that…a piece…not the whole.

The first chapter of the Bible shows us the origin, as well as the purpose, of such a design: "Then God said, 'Let **US** make man in **our** image, in **our** likeness'. So God created man in His own image, in the image of God He created him; male and female He created them" (Genesis 1:26-28).

So who is the **"us"** and **"our"** referred to in verse 26? Why doesn't it say, "Let **Me** make man in **My** image"? Perhaps it is in divine wisdom that God's "image" is not revealed to us as a **"ME"**…but rather as a **"Holy Us-ness"**. God's image includes His position as Creator, as Savior, and as Sustainer of all life. Therefore, He reveals Himself to us as God the Father (revealed in heaven), God the Son, Jesus Christ (God's own flesh and blood revealed on earth), and God the Holy Spirit of Truth (revealed in those who will receive Him).

So although there is but one God, we see Him choosing to reveal Himself through the concept of Holy Union. The value of such Divine Union becomes realized through God's design of human maleness and femaleness…where, when joined together as one, they demonstrate God's own creative abilities. Thus God's value is put into visible expression, becoming recognized and manifested through the intentionally cooperative efforts of His creation!

21

Cooperation

How awesome it is to think of God creating you and me with the specific purpose of being His vessels of power and strength. It is flattering, yet humbling, to understand that God has privileged us to experience the ability that *He* has, by inviting us to become co-creators and co-caretakers with Him and for Him. In His wisdom, however, God has entrusted this experience not just to one of us, but rather He designed it to require the combined abilities of more than just one. And not so surprisingly, this requires cooperation, which leads to unity.

Unity...designed unity...all the parts or elements working together harmoniously...to produce something delightful to all!

God's divine plan certainly contradicts the popular humanistic idea that individual "independence" is the goal. But at the same time it calls for each of us to be individually responsible to assume our part...which requires knowing what our part is...and knowing how our part fits into the whole.

22

The Whole Truth

It's a lot bigger than I am and very tough", explained one man. "No, it's quite flexible, and surely smaller than I", countered another. Then a third voice was heard to insist, "No, no…It's not tough, it's smooth!…And it's certainly not flexible!"

And so we have here…the story of the three blind men describing an elephant…each touching only a part, not the whole and therefore describing only what he had come in contact with personally. "It's a lot bigger than I am and very tough", exclaimed the first blind man as he touched the elephant's body. "No it's quite flexible and surely smaller than I", countered the second blind man as he touched the elephants ear. In the meantime, while touching the elephant's smooth, inflexible tusk, the third blind man continued to insist that the other two were wrong!

And so it is, I think, with so many things in our lives. We understand the essence of something only in the light of our incomplete vision or experience of it. We may come in contact with something we feel is true. So we sincerely and tenaciously cling to our perspective…yet we are not realizing that what we are experiencing is but a part of a much bigger picture.

For many years, much of my own life was lived according to a similarly defective system. I was in my late twenties with some well meaning yet painfully ignorant choices under my belt, before I started separating and questioning various pieces of my own belief system…

because I was beginning to see how incomplete my understanding of life was… and that "sincerity" was not a functional substitute for "accuracy". I had come to realize that while I might sincerely believe that drinking cyanide wouldn't hurt me, the depth of my sincerity would not prevent the reality of consequences!

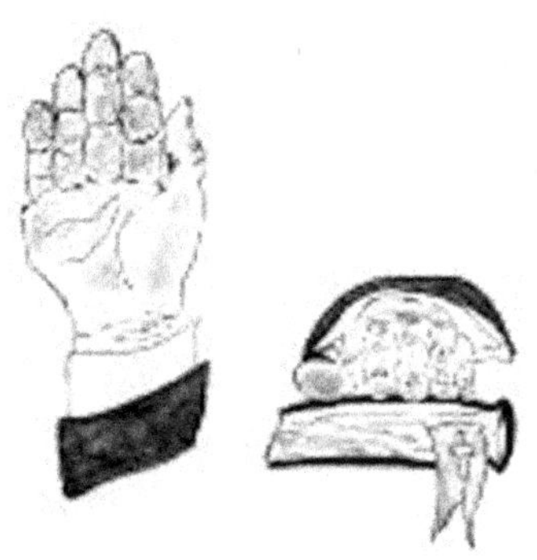

23

Nothing But The Truth

"**D**o you swear to tell the truth, the whole truth, and nothing but the truth, so help you God"? When do we ask this question? Where do we ask this question? And why so we ask this question?

What happens when someone compromises the truth, or just withholds a little of it in order to "self protect"? Isn't it only "natural" for us to try to protect ourselves? Doesn't God Himself *want* us to be protected…*saved*…from harm?

In the first chapter of the book of John, the point is made that the Word of God is God, and that the Word of God is light. It explains that the Word became flesh…took on human form in the person of Jesus Christ. Through the life of Jesus, we are given to see what a life lived in truth looks like. Thus, we are given to see the benevolent attachment of true love. Without the example of Jesus, we would be doomed to the limits of our human perception. Therefore, we would be left to think it appropriate to gratify or protect ourselves any time or way we think it necessary.

What was different about Jesus Christ? Why wasn't His human nature automatically lured and captured by sin? What power did He have going for Him that was more powerful than human will power? What kept Him from compromising the truth in order to gratify or protect "self"?

"I and the Father are One" *(John 10:30)*. "For I have come down from heaven, not to do My own will, but the will of Him who sent Me" *(John 6:38)*. "I can do nothing on My own initiative. As I hear, I judge; and my judgement is just, because I do **not seek** *My own will*, but the will of Him who sent Me" *(John 5:30)*. "For this is the will of My Father, that everyone who beholds the Son and believes in Him, may have eternal life; and I Myself will raise him up on the last day" *(John 6:40)*. "He who believes in Me does not believe in Me, but in Him who sent Me. And he who beholds Me beholds the One who sent Me" *(John 12:44&45)*. "If anyone loves Me, he will keep My word; and My Father will love him, and make Our abode with him. He who does not love Me does not keep My words; and the word which you hear is not Mine, but the Father's who sent Me" *(John 14:23, 24, 21)*.

Interestingly, God warns that intimate disclosure of Himself comes only as we fully commit ourselves to Him. We may want to say to Him, "Show me then I will trust You". But His offer to us is, "Trust Me then I will show you".

While we live in a world that very much advocates physical or emotional intimacy apart from spiritual commitment, we see that in God's design, commitment is not only to proceed, but is, in fact, *required* in true love. And we see that the value or purpose of "true love" or "truth in love"…is that it is our very best and most complete "mutual benefit and protection".

"But I say, walk by the spirit, and you will not carry out the desires of the flesh. For the flesh sets its desires against the Spirit, and the Spirit against the flesh; for these are in opposition to one another, so that you may not do the things that you please".

Galatians 5:16-17

24

The Road To True Contentment

All of mankind was created both flesh and spirit. But apart from our spirit being intimately connected to the Spirit of God, our flesh will live enslaved to its lower nature. And there, our human, less than all knowing appetites, which are prone to self-indulgence, will draw us to self-destruction. Satan seeks to hold us hostage in this prison of self-absorption, while God's Holy Spirit seeks to set us free.

When Jesus Christ allowed His flesh and blood to be crucified on a cross, He revealed the presence of resurrection power...victory over sin's consequence (death). This resurrection power became released through Jesus' cooperative connection with His Heavenly Father. While the ***spirit-of-unholiness seeks to enslave our flesh*** through its powerlessness to say "no", God's Holy Spirit offers or extends Himself to us, bringing us to "know", that is..."to be intimately acquainted" or "united with" the indwelling empowering of His Holiness.

When Christ lives in us as our Savior and Lord, His victory over sin lives in us. A Christian, or Christ-one, is one who has laid down or relinquished his fleshly nature or self-centered will, submitting and committing himself or herself to Jesus, the Christ, the Living Word...the Spirit of Truth and Love.

Because all of us have come from pasts that include sin damage, we may, at times, find it hard to relinquish the self-centered will within, because that is what we have a tendency to depend on for survival. We may be frightened by the thought of Christ shining His

Light of Truth on all the dark corners of our lives. We may want to avoid exposing all the hidden ugliness and pain.

Yet when we come to understand that the purpose of light is to reveal and rescue us from the darkness of defeat, we will be able to experience "Light" as our friend, our ally, our protector. "God's Holy Spirit of Truth" is designed to uncover the ignorance and error that hurts us and hurts others, and offer us a better way. As Christ-ones, we no longer have to resort to illusive and destructive methods, in an effort to protect ourselves or to get our needs met

"But, what if I give up control of my life to the Lord and He doesn't give me what I want", we might be tempted to ask. That is about like saying, "Lord, I want You to be the Lord of my life and I'll tell You just how I want You to do it! But what if God always gave us what we asked for, in stead of what He knows we need?

It was never God's desire that we stumble and fumble our way through life. But we will, until we come to know and trust God's methods and design for life. Only then, as we realize the wisdom in God's incredible and self-sacrificing love, will we find ourselves able to rest securely…by cooperating with Him fully!

"Make me know Thy ways, O'Lord; Teach me Thy paths. Lead me in Thy truth and teach me, For thou art the God of my salvation"...

Psalms 25:4&5

25

Ingesting God's Truth

As a mother, grandmother, and great grandmother, I'm tempted to think that by now I am what I am. But, as I see the lives around me ever growing and changing, I realize that they are seeing my life happening as well. Do they see me growing and changing too? Am I allowing the embryo of God's image in me to become developed…instead of aborted!

I've made mistakes…and I wish I could take them all back! Yet God lovingly reminds me of the value of this journey called life…by empowering me to see and admit my mistakes…which allows them to become a wisdom that those behind me can see…in front of them.

As I attempt to share with others, what God has shared with me over the years, I do so with the hope that you may be encouraged. I pray that you might take a step or steps closer to God…in order to let Him show you your own very specific and unique value. I warn you it won't always be easy…but I can promise you that it will be *eternally* worth it!

Therefore, I would like to invite you to consider trying a little exercise that God taught me. I would like to encourage you to get yourself a notebook, and go back to the beginning of this book and page-by-page, list the scripture references you find. Then, one at a time, day-by-day, look up one of the scriptures in a bible and copy it down in your notebook. Then, write down whatever else comes to your mind as you think about that verse and how it might pertain to your life. Over a period of time, you may be surprised at what God shows you…personally.

On the next page, you will see how God brought me to a similar exercise many years ago. Little did I realize then, that God would use it to teach me…how to hear *His* voice…above all others!

25

Write It Down

"Write it down", I hear in my mind. "But Lord, it's late and I'm tired", I argued. "You will forget the exact wording I'm showing you right now…and if you try to say it your way instead of my way, it won't accomplish what I want it to accomplish", is the unwelcome answer. "Alright", I reply as I get up out of bed and head for my study…"OK Lord, show it to me again and I'll write it down just the way you show me to this time". I'm thinking, … "I know He's right"…but I'm also thinking," I'm apt to be tired in the morning if I don't get this over with quickly. So He talks and I write. And when the talking stops I stop…and go back to bed. As I'm just getting comfortable again, I hear, …"I wasn't finished … I have more to say to you". So back I go to my study. I should know by now that He won't be rushed; that I should sit there at my desk and wait patiently and quietly for Him to finish telling me what He wants me to see. After all, this isn't my first experience like this. As a matter of fact, it's been going on for years…As I study His Word…He shows me His Truth.

The messages vary, but the theme is always the same. "My way, Diane,…My way is what works and I'll show you why"…

26

Unholy Love

It seemed like everywhere I turned, I was faced with it…and each time, an overwhelming emotional stench filled the nostrils of my aching heart. I battled feelings of repulsion, choosing instead to lift my heart to my Lord…trusting Him to calm and enlighten me.

"Something isn't right here, Lord!", I petitioned. "Please help me understand what I'm experiencing!…What is it that is bothering me so? Why am I so bothered by all the offers or admonishings to… love, love, love!?"

"What is being offered you?…And, what is being asked of you?", was the reply. "They say that what they are offering is 'love', Lord. But it doesn't look or feel like **Your** Love. They're asking me to embrace it, Lord. But something feels very…not ok… about it!"

"Your Love is secure…theirs is frightening. Your Love warns and protects…theirs offers my vulnerability to harm. Your Love promotes righteousness…theirs allows and rationalizes sin. They say that it is 'loving' to ignore or over-look sin, Lord. So they want me to embrace that idea in order to accept and console people in their sin. They refuse to see or believe the depth of the pain and loss that sin causes. Their sweet smiles and outstretched arms feel repulsive to me, Lord. Their so called 'love' doesn't have Your smell of sweetness, Lord. It smells fishy! It smells like something tainted…something spoiled!"

"That is because perceptions about 'love' can become distorted", I thought I heard Him explain. "Perversion putrefies. Correction purifies. My Holy Spirit of Truth provides correction…which provides protection" *(1Peter 1:22; 1John 2:3-5; 1John 4:8).*

25

The Truth About Love

When you truly love someone, their welfare or highest gain is the unselfish desire of your heart. You feel for them, and with them, their every joy or pain. You want the very best for them. You want to be able to give them everything that it takes to become all that they can be. If need be, you would give your very life, if it meant saving theirs! That kind of love is powerful, that kind of love is Divine. That kind of love is what God feels for you and me!

The depth of God's love for us was proven by the truth of His willingness to suffer the ultimate pain in order to provide us, His beloved, the ultimate gain! God knew from the beginning what Adam and Eve would do when He created them and entrusted the garden of paradise to their care. He knew right from the start what they (we) would have to go through, and what He Himself would have to suffer, in order to bring us to the Truth, in order to bring us to Himself, in order to bring us to the experience of "True Love". God knew from the beginning what it was going to cost Him to share His Life with us! It would cost Him...***His All***. Yet because of His incredibly unselfish Love for us, God wholeheartedly assumed that sacrificial responsibility!

Those of us who have had the experience of being a parent may be able to identify with the concept of sacrificial parental love. Yet such love is not restricted to parenthood. Because sacrificial love is Divine...and parenthood is but one of many avenues that provides the opportunity to experience it. And as we come to understand the martyrdom or substitutionary death involved in unselfish loving, we begin to realize that the sacrificing of "self" for the sake of another, is the ultimate manifestation or test of true love. And oh how we yearn for such love. And the good news is that it is available to each and every one of us. Because that ultimate manifestation of Love… Divine Love…can be experienced by anyone who comes to realize their own unique preciousness to God!

We need to remember that it was God – our Divine – Heavenly – Father, who created us out of a love that unselfishly relinquished **His Own** Flesh and Blood…in order to provide and protect ours. And, we need to recognize that God's Love isn't like any earthly love we've ever known. Human nature is fallen…imperfect in its ability to love. But God's nature is Divine…Totally Pure, Perfect, and Wise.

Our very existence is by God's design. Only **He** knows just exactly what it takes to bring us to fulfillment. Only **He** is capable of love so perfect and so powerful that it will fill all the yearnings of our mind, heart, body, and soul… because that is what it was designed to do. God knows, and is bringing us to know, that only **He** can fill the hole inside us…Only **He** can make us whole!

27

Whole-ness

"**F**or the mystery of lawlessness is already at work; only He who now restrains will do so until he is taken out of the way. And then that lawless one will be revealed whom the Lord will slay with the breath of His mouth and bring to an end by the appearance of His coming; that is, the one whose coming is in accord with the activity of Satan, with all power and signs and false wonders, and with all the deception of wickedness for *those who perish because they did not receive the love of the truth so as to be saved.* And for this reason God will send upon them, a deluding influence so that they might believe what is false in order that they may all be judged who did not believe the truth, but took pleasure in wickedness. But *we should always give thanks to God for you, brethren beloved by the Lord because God has chosen you from the beginning for salvation…through sanctification by the spirit and faith in the Truth*" (2 Thessalonians 2:7-13).

Whole-ness comes from God's Spirit indwelling us. God designed us to need Him…to complete us. Un-holiness results when we try to function without the leading of God's Holy Spirit. Immaturity, incompletion (un-whole-ness). is where we all start. Whole-ness produces holiness…which is where God designed us to end up (1Peter 1:16). God knows, and wants us to know, that our human nature is vulnerable…easily misled. Therefore, He seeks to show us that human error begins, wherever the believing in Divine Truth ends. Deluding influences, the deception of wickedness, will prevail with those who do not receive the love of the Truth so as to be saved.

Because the reactions of our "human nature" are so automatic or "natural", we may at time, be tempted to feel like we are "trapped" in a bottomless pit which we think we are supposed to climb out of by our own strength or power. But God's design is not that we struggle alone…in an attempt to "prove ourselves". God's design is that we learn to invite Him into our pit of unwholeness …so that He can Lead us out…because only He knows the way!

Inviting God into "our mess" is humbling! We would feel a lot better if we could "clean things up a little" before exposing ourselves to Him. But the truth of the matter is…He already sees and understands our situation better than we do. That's why He offers us His Provision for our condition.

…"And there is no creature hidden from His sight, but all things are open and laid bare to the eyes of Him with whom we have to do. Since we have a Great High Priest who has passed through the heavens, Jesus the Son of God, let us hold fast our confession. *For we do not have a high priest who can not sympathize with our weaknesses*, but one who has been tempted in all things as we are, yet without sin. *Let us; therefore, draw near with confidence to the Throne of Grace, that we may receive mercy and find grace to help in time of need*" (Hebrews 4:13-16).

> *Mercy* (Gr. eleos: *tender compassion accompanied by the desire to help find grace).*
>
> *Grace* (Gr. Charis: *Divine influence upon the heart, and its reflection in the life).*

So just…"REACH OUT" to Him! …And Let Him Take Hold of You!